DO IT FOR YOURSELF

Canadian Cataloguing in Publication Data

Bellows, Mary.
  Do it for yourself

ISBN 0-458-99710-2

1. Dwellings — Maintenance and repair — Amateurs' manuals. I. Title.

TH4817.3.B44 1985   643′.7   C85-099559-0

Design: Jon Eby

Printed and bound in Canada

1 2 3 4   85   89 88 87 86

DO IT FOR YOURSELF

BY MARY BELLOWS

edited by Derek Smith
illustrated by Harvey Booth

METHUEN

Toronto   New York   London   Sydney   Auckland

CONTENTS

ACKNOWLEDGMENTS

To the entire television crew of "Do It For Yourself," especially Elizabeth, François, Randy, Ron, Mike, Jimmy, Gerry, Roger, Barb, Bernie, and Steve, who always made me smile...

To Pat, for hours of dedication...

To Thom Benson for taking a chance...

To John for fun, healthy plants, and for being flexible...

To Henry for giving the pictures life and for always smiling...

To Grant for caring...

To Harvey for giving Zeke, Hoover, and all my words life...

To my trusted friend Zeke, who really knows all the fix-it secrets, and to Hoover, who is learning them...

To Derek, who gave me the courage not to be afraid and the freedom to be myself...

And to my children, Taulene, Mischa, Kendall, and Whitney, who love me just the way I am...

PREFACE

Until that first day when I stepped onto the television set of "Do It For Yourself," my household repairs were relegated to installing light bulbs and changing toilet paper rolls. I could glue, tape, or tie anything together, and I didn't know a nut from a bolt. I owned a hammer, which I used when I hung pictures or cracked walnuts. My screwdriver and pliers were used to open stuck jar lids. A light that didn't work meant call an electrician, a burst pipe meant call a plumber, and a broken chair meant throw it in the garbage! I was terrified by even the thought of having to repair anything. The first time I held a power drill in my hand I screamed and dropped it like a hot potato. Someone told me to pick it up, and that, I guess, was the beginning.

The fix-it secret is attitude. When the first strip of wallpaper that took you twenty minutes to hang falls on the floor, when you break the piece of glass you're trying to install, when you watch the screw you need disappear down the drain, when you break a tile or blow the entire fuse panel, and when it takes you four trips to the store to get the right screwdriver, remember that even the experts make mistakes. Smile a lot. If you're finding it difficult to smile, laugh. This will keep you from throwing your hammer at the wall! When you get ready to repair something for the first time, send everyone in the house, except the dog, out of town. You don't need someone standing over your shoulder, asking you in mid-repair, "Do you really know what you're doing?" You can talk to the dog, and he'll approve of everything you do!

When I was young, my parents used to tell me never to say, "I can't," but to say instead, "I'll try." If you are always willing to try something new, you'll not only experience that certain sense of adventure that accompanies doing things for the first time, but you'll also be overwhelmed by the feeling of accomplishment when you complete the task successfully.

This book is for those of you who want to fix things around the house, but are afraid to try. Just remember:

If I can do it, so can you!

BASIC TOOLS

When a hammer, a screwdriver, and a pair of pliers replace a shoe, a knife, and kitchen tongs, or how to help make every repair easy and fun. Sometimes you need all the help you can get!

HAMMER Hammers come in various sizes, shapes, and weight categories. Me, I like a 13-oz. claw hammer. Get one that feels comfortable in your hand. If aesthetics are important, tie a ribbon on it. It's now officially yours.

SCREWDRIVERS One of every size and shape imaginable. Every screw you meet on the repair road is a potential surprise. The three basic types are: slotted, Philips, and Robertson. Know this and you can talk intelligently to the person at the store. Ask for these for Christmas instead of new pots and pans.

TAPE MEASURE Unfortunately, the ability to measure doesn't come with it, nor do instructions. A 12′ tape measure should be adequate. Of course, the first thing you measure will be 12′6″.

UTILITY KNIFE One that retracts into a metal case—it'll save on bandages. Good-bye, kitchen knife. It doesn't even slice tomatoes anyway, so how can it ever cut wallpaper, screen, or vinyl flooring?

SLIP-JOINT PLIERS The choice is yours. They come in plain old ordinary or in what appears to be more complicated but probably isn't. Use whatever is most comfortable and easy to handle. Practice in the store. Just don't get caught as you go around loosening things.

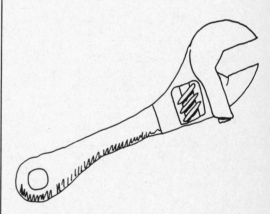

NEEDLE-NOSE LIERS Small pliers with a long, pointy snout. These are wonderful for small bits, pieces, and tight spots, like when you drop something down the drain.

ADJUSTABLE WRENCHES One small, 1 medium, and 1 large. Each size needs a backup because the nut you want to remove is invariably just a hair too big to fit the wrench in your hand. If you want to be economical, a 12″ wrench should do it, until it doesn't. Then you need the backups.

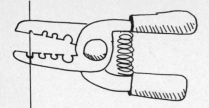

WIRE STRIPPERS Essential and efficient. Never use a knife; remember, it's too dull anyway. Use these once and you'll never even think about a knife. All it takes is a little practice to figure out which hole the wire goes in.

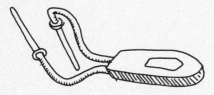

CIRCUIT TESTER Your cheapest and best electrical friend. When it lights up, it means "don't touch." If it doesn't light up, it means "touch, spend, and repair."

COMBINATION SQUARE A real 4-in-1. It measures angles, is a level and a ruler, and at the very least it's a straight edge. Get the person at the store to show you how all the parts work. This is a real "show me" tool.

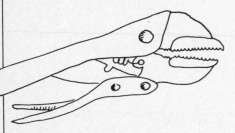

VISE GRIPS Optional. To some the world's handiest tool, to me a perceptual puzzle. These should come with instructions or with someone to show you how they work. Or better still, someone to work them for you.

ASSORTMENT OF PENCILS, CRAYONS, PERMANENT MARKERS, SCREWS, NAILS, NUTS, BOLTS, POPSICLE STICKS, TAPE, WIRE, STRING, AND BANDAGES If you never throw anything away, you already have some of these. When you clean the house you'll find the rest.

DRILL AND ASSORTED BITS A drill won't fit in your toolbox, but it certainly makes neat holes. A rechargeable, cordless drill is best so you're not forever tripping over or sorting out miles of electrical cord.

HANDSAW Your choice, but sharp is better than dull and rusty. A combination crosscut and rip saw is best. (I was told to say this.) A giant saw isn't necessarily handy, and an expensive saw that's going to hang in the garage isn't at all necessary. Don't get one that's unwieldy; operating a saw is difficult enough.

GLUE For when you've had it with the hammer, the screwdriver, and the pliers.

TOOLBOX Buy one that's on sale. It's better than a shoe box and more organized than your junk drawer.

LOCK For the toolbox. Just remember where you put the key.

IF YOU SHARE YOUR TOOLS, TIE RIBBONS ON THEM. THEN YOU DON'T NEED TO WORRY ABOUT LOCKS AND KEYS.

When buying tools, always buy something that is comfortable in your hand. Handgrips are important—you'll get fewer blisters. Big, heavy tools may look official, but they can be unwieldy, and who needs a doorstop in the shape of a jigsaw? Buy a screwdriver that costs $5.00 and not a whole set for $1.49. Inexpensive screwdrivers have soft tips, and after the first few screws you'll have an icepick. Buy a good-quality drill too. It will last forever. And only buy the tools you know you can and will use!

13

ELECTRICAL

*One step beyond
changing a light bulb.*

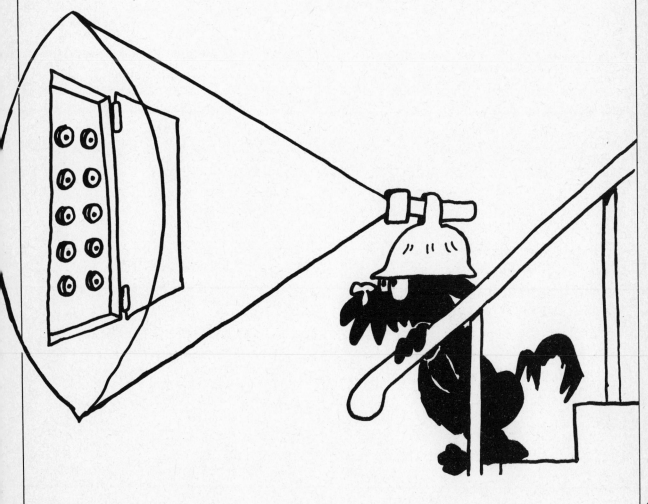

REPLACING A PLUG ON AN ELECTRICAL CORD

What to do if you don't have the money to buy a new whatever.

1 **MAKE SURE THE NEW PLUG IS COMPATIBLE WITH THE CORD.**
When in doubt, take the whole thing to the store.

2 **CUT OFF THE DEAD PLUG AND A SHORT PIECE OF THE DEAD WIRE.**
Don't throw it away. You never know—you might be able to use it for something.

3 **REMOVE THE INNER UNIT FROM THE PLUG CASING.**
This takes a certain amount of ingenuity, but don't give up. They can be separated.

4 **INSERT THE WIRE THROUGH THE PLUG CASING.**
This is the most important step in the entire operation. You don't want to have to do it all over again. If you do, laugh—it helps!

5 **SLIT THE CORD 1/2″ BETWEEN THE WIRES.**
Use scissors (not your good ones) or wire strippers. Don't ever use a knife or you might make an unexpected trip to the hospital.

6 **STRIP 1/2″ OF INSULATION FROM EACH WIRE, MAKING SURE THAT THE COPPER STRANDS ARE NOT FRAYED.**
Practice a lot and hope that whatever you're working on comes with a long cord.

7 **TWIST THE COPPER STRANDS OF EACH WIRE TOGETHER**
—not together together but together separately—**CLOCKWISE.** This may be the most time-consuming step; deciding which way is clockwise could take all day.

8 **LOOP THE WIRES CLOCKWISE AROUND THE TERMINAL SCREWS ON THE INNER UNIT.**
If it's a 3-pronged plug, make sure the ground wire is connected to the ground terminal. This is usually a green screw, but if not, look for the screw that's connected to the fat prong. Two prongs are skinny and 1 is fat.

9 **TIGHTEN THE SCREWS AND MAKE SURE THAT NONE OF THE STRANDS FROM 1 TERMINAL TOUCH THOSE ON THE OTHER.**
The plug could short out, turn black, or disintegrate before your very eyes.

10 **REPLACE THE PLUG CASING.**
You're almost there.

11 If you've got this far and you have this

left over, go back to Step 4 and start again. If you haven't...

12 **CROSS YOUR FINGERS AND PLUG IT IN.**

REPLACING A PLUG WITH A QUICK FIX-IT PLUG

This is good only for skinny little 2-wire electrical cords.

1 **CLEANLY CUT OFF THE DEAD PLUG AND A PIECE OF THE DEAD WIRE.**

2 **DO NOT SLIT THE WIRES.**
Hooray, no tools!

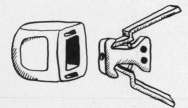

3 **REMOVE THE INNER UNIT FROM THE PLUG CASING.**
Good luck, keep fiddling.

4 **INSERT THE WIRE THROUGH THE PLUG CASING.**
This is the "don't forget" step.

5 **SPREAD THE BLADES APART AND PUSH THE WIRE INTO THE BACK OF THE PLUG AS FAR AS POSSIBLE.**

6 **SQUEEZE THE BLADES TOGETHER AND PRESS THE INNER UNIT FIRMLY INTO THE CASING.**
It will take more effort than "press" indicates—something like brute force.

7 Remember the "don't forget" step? If you have one of these

left over, go back to the beginning—and keep smiling!

8 **THIS IS WHAT IT SHOULD LOOK LIKE...**

...SORT OF.

Once again you can choose to call it by either name. I chose ''outlet'' because it's easier to spell. You know you have to replace one when you're busily making breakfast one morning. You zip the bread into the toaster, push down the pop-up lever, and race off to make the eggs. You get everyone and everything to the table— the juice, the bacon, the eggs, the jam— and no toast. You look back at the toaster, the lever is still down. Look into the toaster, the bread is still bread. Fiddle with the lever, it goes up and down. Fiddle with the plug, it's in there nice and snug.

Now what? Just as you're about to throw the bread on the table and the toaster in the garbage, you try another outlet. Hooray, it works—toast! As you sit there surveying the dirty dishes, you try to figure out what could be wrong with the outlet and why you didn't get any toast and everyone else did.

1 **CHECK THE FUSE BOX OR CIRCUIT BREAKER.**
If they're all okay, decide whether you want to do the dishes first or go to the store to get a circuit tester. If you're like me, you'll do the dishes. I always do first what I know is a sure thing. That way I approach repairs with a certain amount of confidence. In school I majored in laundry, vacuuming, dishes, and procrastinating. Procrastinating is really putting something off until you feel better about doing it.

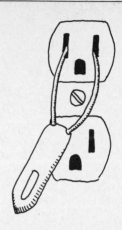

2 **GO TO THE STORE AND GET A CIRCUIT TESTER.**
Cheap works just as well as expensive. **PUT THE PRONGS OF THE TESTER INTO THE OUTLET SLOTS. IF THE LIGHT ON THE TESTER DOESN'T GO ON** and you know the power is still on, **THE OUTLET IS BROKEN, DAMAGED, OR DEAD.**

3 **TURN OFF THE POWER TO THE DEAD OUTLET.**
If your fuse box or the circuit breakers aren't marked, you have to turn off the main power supply. This is usually done by tripping a lever located on the side of the fuse box. Tape the lever down—this is not the time for someone to notice the power is off, trip the lever on, and inadvertently send you right into next week. The thought of this happening and the possibility of the ice cream in your freezer turning into soup will make you put ''marking the fuses or breakers'' on your list of rainy day activities.

4 **REMOVE THE OUTLET COVER PLATE AND PLACE THE PRONGS OF THE CIRCUIT TESTER AGAINST THE BARE ENDS OF THE BLACK AND WHITE WIRES AT THE POINTS WHERE THEY ARE ATTACHED TO THE OUTLET.**
Put 1 prong of the tester on the wire attached to the brass terminal and 1 prong on the wire attached to the corresponding silver terminal. If there is a wire connected to the other brass terminal, test it in the same manner. However—there's always a ''however''—you might see 1 wire attached to a brass terminal and 1 wire attached to the—how do you say ''not corresponding?''—how about opposite silver terminal. Test these, 1 prong on each wire. If the outlet is back-wired, you have to wait until Step 7 to make the test. **THE BULB IN THE TESTER SHOULD NOT LIGHT.** If it does, go down to the fuse panel and see what it was you turned off.

5 **ONCE YOU KNOW THERE'S NO ELECTRICITY IN THE OUTLET, AND BEFORE YOU START REMOVING ANYTHING ELSE, GET A PENCIL AND A PIECE OF PAPER.**
Make a diagram of what you are going to take apart. This is essential for getting it all back together again.

6 **LOOK AT THE TOP AND BOTTOM OF THE OUTLET FOR THE MOUNTING SCREWS THAT HOLD THE OUTLET IN THE BOX.**
Usually the screws are inserted in what look like metal ears. They are in fact called *plaster ears*. Having always called parts *thingamajigs*, I am now preoccupied with their proper names. *Plaster ears* was a real find.

LOOSEN BUT DO NOT REMOVE THESE SCREWS, which are the world's longest, **FROM THE PLASTER EARS AND PICK UP THE LITTLE FIBER WASHERS THAT WILL FALL ON THE FLOOR.** They hold the screws in the ears. Make a note to remember to put them back. Leftovers, no matter how small, mean you get to go back and do something all over again. I don't really understand why you have to leave the screws in the ears, unless it's so you know where they are when you get to Step 16.

7 **PULL THE OUTLET TOWARD YOU OUT OF THE BOX WITHOUT DISCONNECTING ANY WIRES.**
''Pull'' is almost always ''tug.''

8 **MAKE A DIAGRAM OF EXACTLY WHAT YOU ARE LOOKING AT.**
Draw the front, sides, and bottom—anything that helps you remember exactly what wire went where. No matter how many wires are running around in there, the new outlet must be attached in exactly the same way. Now if you have a camera...

19

9 IF THE OUTLET IS *SIDE-WIRED*, LOOSEN THE TERMINAL SCREWS AND REMOVE THE WIRES. IF THE OUTLET IS *BACK-WIRED*, REMOVE THE WIRES BY PRESSING THE TIP OF A SCREWDRIVER INTO THE RELEASE SLOT AND PULLING THE WIRES STRAIGHT OUT.

10 TAKE THE DEAD OUTLET TO THE STORE AND GET EITHER AN EXACT OR AN UPGRADED REPLACEMENT.
It is important to replace an outlet with 2 slotted plugs with a 3-slotted grounded outlet. It is also essential that the new outlet have the same specifications as the old one. Stamped on the outlet are things like AL-CU, which means the outlet can be used with aluminum or copper wiring, or CO-ALR, which means your guess is as good as mine. Whatever letters are stamped on the outlet, they all have to do with keeping the house wiring and the outlet compatible. There is also something like this: 15A/125V. This indicates the maximum amperage and voltage for the outlet. You can see why it might be a good idea to ask at the store.

11 WITH THE NEW OUTLET AND YOUR DRAWING IN HAND,
think about the piece of toast you're going to have for lunch. CHECK THE ENDS OF THE WIRES; the solid copper wire should not be nicked. If it is, put down the outlet and drawing, forget about your toast, and find your wire strippers.

12 USING WIRE STRIPPERS, CUT OFF THE NICKED PIECE OF WIRE. FOR A SIDE-WIRED OUTLET, STRIP ENOUGH INSULATION TO ALLOW THE BARE END OF THE WIRE TO WRAP 3/4 OF THE WAY AROUND THE TERMINAL. MAKE A LOOP IN THE BARE END OF THE WIRE—

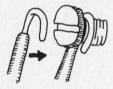

you can do this by putting the bare wire into a hole in the wire stripper and twisting the stripper (no comment)—**TO GO CLOCK-WISE AROUND THE TERMINAL SCREW;**

as the screw is tightened, it helps close the loop. **IF YOU'RE REPLACING A BACK-WIRED OUTLET, A GAUGE ON THE BACK OF THE OUTLET TELLS YOU HOW MUCH INSULATION TO REMOVE.**

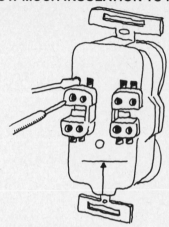

Here you don't have to worry about loops or twisting strippers. Be careful when cutting and stripping these wires not to remove too much wire. You can't make short wire longer. Short is short, and if you're not careful, you'll end up with a nice, neat loop on a stubby little piece of wire that won't reach the terminal screw.

13 WITH YOUR DRAWING IN FRONT OF YOU, ATTACH THE WIRES TO THE NEW OUTLET.
If the outlet is side-wired, make sure the wires go clockwise around the terminal screws. The brass terminal screws are for the black or red wires, and the silver terminal screws are for the white wires. The green screw on the bottom or end of the outlet is for the ground wire. If the outlet is back-wired, the wires are inserted into the holes on the back of the outlet **EXACTLY THE SAME WAY YOU TOOK THEM OFF THE OLD OUTLET.** Your drawing is now your key to success. If it isn't all you hoped it would be, don't panic. Smile, maybe it will help.

THIS IS WHAT YOU MIGHT HAVE RUN INTO:

AN END-OF-THE-RUN OUTLET.
Only 1 large cable enters the box. The black wire is attached to the brass terminal screw, and the white wire is attached to the silver terminal screw. The bare copper wire (ground wire) is attached to the green termi-

nal screw on the bottom or end of the outlet. Hope for this one—it's easiest.

A MIDDLE-OF-THE-RUN OUTLET.
Two large cables enter the box. Each cable has 3 wires—a black, a white, and a bare copper wire (the green or ground wire). If you see a red wire, pretend it's black and connect each black wire to a brass terminal screw on the outlet and each white wire to a silver terminal screw. Attach one 4″ green jumper wire to a screw on the back of the box. Attach a 4″ green jumper wire to the green screw on the outlet. Connect both jumper wires and both bare copper cable wires together with a wire cap, a big, fat wire cap that will hold 4 wires. You'll have fun trying to shove all of this back into the box, and I do mean shove.

A SPLIT OUTLET.
Usually found in the kitchen, where each plug in the outlet is wired separately because most kitchen appliances draw a lot of power. You can tell this is what you have if the metal tab on the brass terminal side between the two plugs has been removed. Break off the same tab on the replacement outlet and rewire the outlet exactly as the old one was wired.

14 **NOW AFTER ALL THAT READING AND WIRING OF 1 KIND OR ANOTHER, IT'S TIME TO PUT EVERYTHING BACK TO-GETHER AGAIN**
and have that piece of toast, which has now turned into a triple-decker sandwich because you're starving.

15 **PUSH (THIS COULD BE "SHOVE") THE NEWLY WIRED OUTLET BACK INTO THE BOX.**
Make sure that any excess wire is behind the outlet.

16 **INSERT THE SCREWS THAT HOLD THE OUTLET IN THE BOX** (don't forget the fiber washers) **THROUGH THE PLASTER EARS AND TIGHTEN THEM.**
This is easier said than done. You are now holding the outlet that wants to spring out of the box with 1 hand. You are holding the screw in the other hand. What do you use to hold the screwdriver? Your toes? You'll think of something.

17 REPLACE THE COVER PLATE AND TURN ON THE POWER.

If you have to trip the main power-supply lever, it's a good idea not to stand directly in front of the fuse panel when you're turning the power on. A surge of power runs through the fuse box in the second that you trip the lever. This is a "just in case" safety hint.

18 WITH THE POWER ON, PLACE THE PRONGS OF THE CIRCUIT TESTER INTO THE SLOTS OF EACH PLUG IN THE OUTLET. IF THE TESTER DOES NOT LIGHT, YOU SHOULD CALL AN ELECTRICIAN BECAUSE EITHER YOUR HANDIWORK OR THE CIRCUIT IS FAULTY.

If the light goes on, proceed to Step 19 with gusto.

19 PLUG THE TOASTER INTO THE NEW OUTLET, PUT IN THE BREAD, PUSH DOWN THE POP-UP LEVER, AND CHEER WHEN THE BREAD COMES BACK TOAST.

Make a sandwich, turn the soupy ice cream in your freezer into a milkshake, and enjoy feeling good about what you've just accomplished.

HELPFUL HINT

IF YOUR FUSES OR CIRCUIT BREAKERS AREN'T MARKED, TURN ON YOUR RADIO—the plug-in variety, battery-operated won't work—LOUD, GO TO THE ELECTRICAL PANEL, AND EITHER REMOVE FUSES OR TRIP BREAKERS UNTIL THE RADIO GOES OFF. You've found one. TEST EACH OUTLET THIS WAY AND MARK FUSES AND BREAKERS AS YOU GO.

TO TEST LIGHT SWITCHES, TURN ON ALL THE LIGHTS IN THE HOUSE. GO TO THE PANEL AND REMOVE A FUSE OR TRIP A BREAKER. RUN AROUND THE HOUSE TO FIND THE LIGHT THAT WENT OFF and hope it isn't just the bulb burning out. After all this running around, you'll wish you had a helper.

These are often called *single-pole switches* by the people who write electrical textbooks. They are the most common kind of switches, and they can last for 20 years, unless it's in my house, where nothing lasts for 20 years. They are easy to replace once you get used to the idea that with the power off you really can't do any harm either to the house or to yourself. It's definitely a daytime job; you need to see what you're doing, and it's a whole lot easier *not* to have someone standing over your shoulder holding a flashlight and asking, "Do you really know what you're doing?" If this is the first time you've taken off a switch plate, do it when the "help" is out. You can repeat the whole operation for the family once you feel more confident.

1 BUY A LOVELY NEW REPLACEMENT SWITCH.

Why make the replacement dull and ordinary? No one will notice what you did. They'll just think that the switch magically decided to work after 5 years. The markings stamped on the new switch must match those stamped on the old one, so you may

have to wait until Step 8 before you go shopping. **AND BUY A CIRCUIT TESTER**—not a fancy one, just one that lets you know where the electricity isn't.

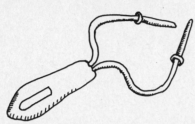

2 **TURN OFF THE POWER TO THE ROOM THAT'S GETTING THE NEW SWITCH.**
If you really aren't sure which fuse or breaker is which, turn off the main power supply. It's usually the lever located on the side of the electrical panel. Before you pull down the lever, get in the habit of standing away from the panel. Nothing will happen when you turn the power off, but it's a good idea not to be in front of the panel when you turn the power on again. There's a lot of power going through there with 1 flip of a lever. This suggestion has to do with safety and my healthy respect for electricity. **TAPE THE LEVER DOWN.** It won't spring up again, but if the ''help'' comes home, they won't help you by turning it back on while you have a handful of wires.

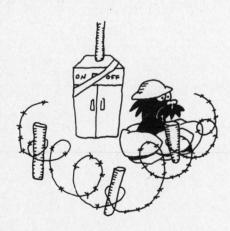

3 **WITH THE SWITCH IN THE OFF POSI-TION** (it's reassuring) **UNSCREW THE SWITCH COVER PLATE.**
So far, so good.

4 **LOOSEN THE SCREWS IN THE MOUNT-ING STRAP**—either a single metal strap with a single screw or *plaster ears*, which are really metal with a screw in each ear—**AT THE TOP AND BOTTOM OF THE SWITCH. THEY HOLD THE SWITCH IN THE METAL BOX UNTIL YOU CAN PULL THE SWITCH OUT OF THE BOX.**
The screws should not come out of either the mounting straps or the plaster ears because they are held in place by little fiber washers. More often than not, however, the screws do come out, and the tiny washers fall on the floor. Don't panic. Just put them in a safe place until you're reassembling.

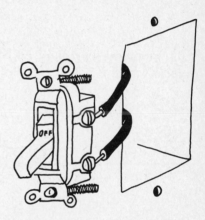

5 **HOLD THE MOUNTING STRAPS OR EARS AT THE TOP AND BOTTOM OF THE SWITCH AND PULL THE SWITCH OUT OF THE BOX UNTIL THE WIRES ARE FULLY EXTENDED.**
Don't worry—it won't fall out on the floor or come off in your hands. If it does, somebody goofed—not you, somebody else.

6 **TO MAKE SURE THE POWER IS REALLY OFF, PLACE 1 PROBE OF THE CIRCUIT TESTER ON THE METAL SHELL OF THE SWITCH BOX AND THE OTHER PROBE ON EACH OF THE BRASS TERMINALS.**
If the light goes on, you either removed the wrong fuse or tripped the wrong lever. It's back to the panel to try again. When in doubt, go back to Step 2 and turn off the main power supply. When the power to the switch is off, the light on the tester will not go on. **IF THE SWITCH HAS PUSH-IN TERMI-**

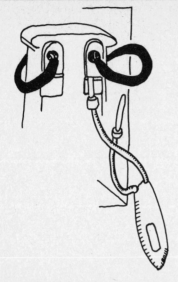

NALS (BACK-WIRED) INSERT 1 PROBE INTO EACH RELEASE SLOT WHILE THE OTHER PROBE IS TOUCHING THE METAL SHELL OF THE BOX. Never leave out this step; it could save you from a nasty zap.

7 GET A PENCIL AND PAPER.
Draw a picture of what you see going on in the box and how the wires are connected to the switch. This removes a certain amount of uncertainty about how it all goes back together and stops you from giving up at this point.

LEGEND

white wire	————
black wire	▬▬▬▬
red wire	∼∼∼∼∼
green wire	⅏⅏⅏⅏
copper wire	∼∼∼∼∼∼

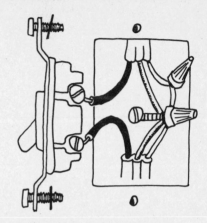

MIDDLE-OF-THE-RUN WIRING.
Two large cables enter the box; each cable has a black wire, a white wire, and a bare copper wire. If you find a red wire, don't worry—it's really a black one. The black wires are the "hot" wires, and they are attached to the switch terminals. The white wires are neutral and are connected with a wire cap. The bare copper wires are ground wires, and they, too, are connected with a wire cap. Never disturb any capped wires when installing a new switch; leave them alone.

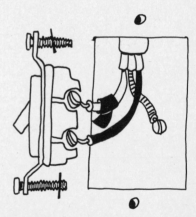

SWITCH-LOOP WIRING.
Only 1 cable enters the box. The black wire and the white wire are connected to the switch. Here the white wire is "hot" and should be marked with a piece of black electrical tape or black permanent marker. If it's not marked, you can do it. The bare copper wire should be attached to the back of the box.

8 | **REMOVE THE SWITCH.**
You have your drawing, so you can take the switch apart with confidence. If the switch is side-wired, loosen the terminal screws and remove the wires. If it's back-wired, the wires poke into the back of the switch. Press the tip of a screwdriver or the end of a stiff wire into the release slot and pull the wires free at the same time—a bit like rubbing your head and patting your stomach at the same time.

9 | **CHECK THE ENDS OF THE WIRES TO MAKE SURE THEY ARE NOT NICKED.**

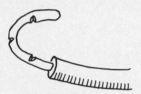

Any nicks could make the wire weak, so **IF THEY ARE NICKED, YOU HAVE TO RE-STRIP THE WIRES.** See Step 12 in the section, "Replacing a Wall Outlet or Receptacle." I once decided not to bother restripping the wires, and just as I got the switch screwed back into the box, both wires snapped off at the terminal screws before

my very eyes. Save yourself a little unnecessary aggravation; restrip the wires, and if you can, back-wire the switch. Then you can forget all about "loop making."

10 | **TO INSTALL THE NEW SWITCH, POSITION IT VERTICALLY SO THAT IT IS OFF WHEN THE SWITCH LEVER IS DOWN AND ON WHEN THE LEVER IS UP** (unless on and off are more important to you than up and down) **AND CONNECT THE 2 "HOT" WIRES TO THE TERMINALS.**
The wires should go on the new switch exactly the same way they came off the old switch. Have any doubts? Look at your drawing—or mine.

11 | **PUSH THE SWITCH BACK INTO THE OUTLET BOX AND TUCK ANY EXCESS WIRE BEHIND THE SWITCH.**

12 | **INSERT THE MOUNTING SCREWS INTO THE MOUNTING STRAPS OR PLASTER EARS ON THE NEW SWITCH AND PUT THOSE TINY FIBER WASHERS ON THE SCREWS TO HOLD THEM ONTO THE STRAPS.**
Hope you put the washers in a safe place, and hope you can remember where the safe place was.

13 | **INSERT THE MOUNTING SCREWS INTO THE CORRESPONDING HOLES IN THE OUTLET BOX AND TIGHTEN THEM.**

14 | **REPLACE THE SWITCH COVER PLATE.**
Stifle your urge to cheer. You're not quite finished.

15 | **TURN ON THE POWER SUPPLY.**
If it was the main panel lever that you tripped, remember to stand away from the box when you turn it on.

16 | **GO BACK TO THE NEW SWITCH** (you could be running at this point if you're anything like me) **AND FLIP IT ON.**
You'll be so excited when it finally turns on a

light that you'll want to flip it on and off a few times. Go ahead, do it—it'll make you feel wonderful!

17. WAIT FOR THAT FIRST "HEY, WHO PUT IN THE NEW SWITCH? AND IT WORKS."

You will absolutely love saying, "I did," and now you can take it all apart and put it back together for everyone with real finesse.

POSSIBLE SWITCHES YOU MAY RUN INTO:

3-WAY, 4-WAY, AND DOUBLE-POLE SWITCHES.

How to recognize what you have when you get to Step 5 in "Replacing a Wall Switch" and it looks nothing like the single-pole switch I described.

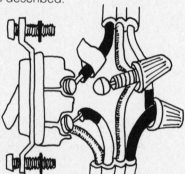

3-WAY SWITCH.

It has 3 terminals. Two are the same color, and 1 is always different: 1 black and 2 brass, 1 copper and 2 silver, or 2 brass and 1 copper. Before removing this switch to replace it, put a piece of tape on the wire that is attached to the different-colored terminal so that you know which wire goes to the different-colored terminal on the new switch. Three-way switches are used in pairs to control a light or receptacle from 2 different locations, like a light at the top of the stairs. You can turn it on at the top and at the bottom so you won't have to go stubbing your toes up the stairs in the dark.

4-WAY SWITCH.

It has 4 brass-colored terminals, and it works in conjunction with 3-way switches to control a light or outlet from 3 or more locations. The switch itself has no "on" or "off" markings. Make sure that when you uncover one of these, your drawing of the wiring is better than ever. Or you could take a picture with

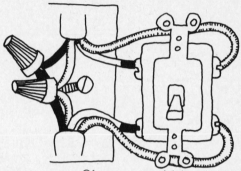

your camera. Of course, you'd then have to take the rest of the pictures on the roll—that could take a month—get the film to the lab, have it developed and processed, and by the time the picture is in your hand, you will have either forgotten why you were replacing that switch or replaced another switch altogether.

DOUBLE-POLE SWITCH.

This is sometimes used to control 240-volt appliances. It can be mistaken for a 4-way switch because it also has 4 brass-colored terminals, but unlike the 4-way switch, it does have "on" and "off" markings.

Note: To replace any of the above switches, make sure the wiring goes on the replacement switch *exactly* the same way it came off the old switch. Make sure that whatever is stamped on the old switch is also stamped on the replacement.

HELPFUL HINT
IF YOU EVER HAVE ANY DOUBTS ABOUT DOING ELECTRICAL WORK, CALL AN ELECTRICIAN AND ASK ADVICE. IF YOU HAVE ANY QUESTIONS ABOUT ELECTRICAL CODES, CALL THE TOWN BYLAW OFFICE. BETTER YET, MAKE FRIENDS WITH AN ELECTRICIAN!

INSTALLING A DIMMER SWITCH

You'll wish you had one when you send the kids off to your mother-in-law's for the weekend, organize a cozy candlelit dinner for two, slip into something other than your blue jeans, put on some lovely soft music, and just as you're about to light the candles you realize there aren't any, not even the stubby ones left over from the Halloween pumpkins. The beacon blazing from the ceiling sends you from the dining room. You settle down to dinner by the light of the television set. That's Friday night gone—maybe Saturday? Wanting desperately to match the light level with the mood you're trying to create, you slip back into your blue jeans early Saturday morning to see what you can do.

1 TURN OFF THE POWER SUPPLY TO THE ROOM.
If you don't know which fuses or circuit breakers are for what room, trip the main power-supply lever on the side of the electrical panel. Think first: is any part of your gourmet dinner for two in the freezer? **TAPE DOWN THE LEVER.** Think of an outdoor activity to keep the person you're planning this for occupied. No power means no TV, no stereo, no power tools. How about washing the car?

2 RETURN TO THE SWITCH. MAKE SURE IT'S IN THE OFF POSITION (for luck) AND REMOVE THE SWITCH COVER PLATE.
Glance occasionally at the searchlight overhead; it will do wonders for your determination.

3 LOOSEN THE LONG (and I do mean long) SCREWS IN EITHER THE MOUNTING STRAP OR THE *PLASTER EARS* LOCATED AT THE TOP AND BOTTOM OF THE SWITCH, AND GRAB THE TINY FIBER WASHERS THAT HOLD THESE SCREWS IN PLACE AS THEY HEAD FOR THE FLOOR ONCE THE SCREWS LEAVE THE SWITCH BOX.
The idea is to try to leave the screws and washers in the old switch for safekeeping. If they come out, don't worry. Just don't lose them—the new switch doesn't come with new screws.

4 HOLD ONTO THE MOUNTING STRAP OR PLASTER EARS AND PULL THE SWITCH OUT OF THE METAL BOX.
Don't let what you see give you apoplexy. Just take another look at what's hanging from the ceiling.

5 TEST THE SWITCH WITH A CIRCUIT TESTER BY TOUCHING 1 PRONG OF THE TESTER TO THE METAL BOX AND THE OTHER PRONG TO EACH TERMINAL. IF THE TESTER DOESN'T LIGHT, IT'S SAFE. IF THE SWITCH IS BACK-WIRED, TOUCH 1 PRONG TO THE METAL BOX AND INSERT THE OTHER PRONG INTO THE RELEASE SLOTS.
If you don't have a circuit tester, read Step 6 and then get one at the store when you're getting the dimmer switch. I'm saving you a trip to the store.

6 TAKE A GOOD LOOK AT WHAT YOU'VE UNCOVERED AND GET A PENCIL AND

PAPER.

Artist or not, **YOU ARE GOING TO DRAW A DIAGRAM OF EXACTLY WHAT YOU SEE. LABEL IT.** The person at the store may not be able to make head or tail of your picture but will understand the words. **IF IT'S A SINGLE-POLE SWITCH,** 2 black wires are attached to the only 2 terminal screws on the switch.

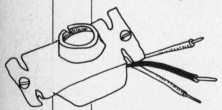

Or if it's a back-wired switch, the 2 wires are inserted in the back, and you'll be off to the store to buy a **SINGLE-POLE DIMMER. IF IT'S A 3-WAY SWITCH,** it has 3 terminal screws. Put a piece of tape on the wire attached to the different terminal (2 screws are 1 color, and 1 screw is a different color); you'll need to

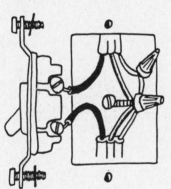

buy a **3-WAY DIMMER. WRITE DOWN ANY AND ALL MARKINGS STAMPED ON THE SWITCH.** The person at the store has to know all this in order to sell you a dimmer with the same wiring requirements as the old switch.

7 **MAKE ABSOLUTELY EVERYTHING OFF LIMITS**—"don't touch" signs are great—**AND GO TO THE STORE, DRAWING IN HAND, TO BUY THE NEW DIMMER SWITCH.**

The car will be only half washed, but take it anyway. Suggest mowing the lawn (only if the mower isn't electric) or cleaning out the garage—with a broom.

8 **BUY A DIMMER SWITCH, A CIRCUIT TESTER,** if you didn't have one, **AND A CANDLE,** just in case.

9 At home again, return the half-washed car. The garage is now cleaner than the car. Just in case, check the power. The lever is still taped down. Test the switch. No light in the tester, and you didn't leave your Rembrandt at the store. You're all set. Take the new dimmer out of the package and with 1 last look at the ceiling beacon, smile. **LOOSEN THE TERMINAL SCREWS ON THE SWITCH, OR IF IT'S BACK-WIRED, PRESS THE TIP OF A SCREWDRIVER INTO THE RELEASE SLOTS AND REMOVE THE WIRES.**

10 **IF THE SWITCH WAS WIRED TO TERMINAL SCREWS, CUT THE "LOOPS" OFF THE ENDS OF THE WIRES AND WITH WIRE STRIPPERS, STRIP THE INSULATION TO MATCH THE STRIPPED ENDS OF THE DIMMER LEADS.**

Back-wired switch wires should not need to be restripped unless they are nicked.

11 **REMOVE THE KNOB FROM THE DIMMER BY PULLING IT STRAIGHT OFF THE KNURLED POST.**

Don't lose it, or you'll get to use that "just in case" candle.

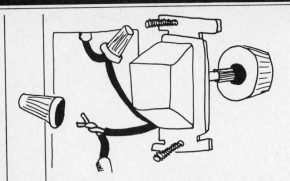

12 FOR A SINGLE-POLE DIMMER, WIRE EACH DIMMER LEAD WIRE—there are 2 hanging from the dimmer—**TO EACH OF THE "HOT" WIRES THAT WERE ATTACHED TO THE SWITCH BY TWISTING THE LEAD WIRES CLOCKWISE AROUND THE SOLID COPPER WIRES AND SCREWING A WIRE CAP, CLOCKWISE, FIRMLY ON EACH SET OF CONNECTED WIRES.**
The wire cap is a little house that covers the connection and ensures that the wires won't separate.

13 IF THE DIMMER IS REPLACING A 3-WAY SWITCH, IT WILL HAVE 2 SAME-COLORED LEAD WIRES AND 1 OF A DIFFERENT COLOR. ATTACH THE DIFFERENT-COLORED LEAD WIRE ON THE DIMMER TO THE WIRE THAT WAS ATTACHED TO THE DIFFERENT TERMINAL ON THE SWITCH—the one you taped—**AND ATTACH THE 2 SAME-COLORED LEAD WIRES ON THE DIMMER TO THE WIRES THAT WERE ATTACHED TO THE SIMILAR SWITCH TERMINALS.**

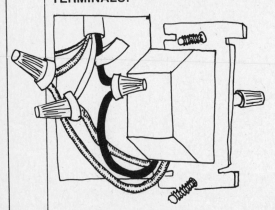

In other words, attach the oddball lead wire

to the oddball switch wire and the similar lead wire to the similar switch wires. **ATTACH ALL WIRES AS DESCRIBED IN STEP 12 AND DON'T FORGET THE WIRE CAPS.**

14 PUSH THE DIMMER, and all of its various wires and caps, **INTO THE BOX. MAKE SURE THE WIRES ARE BEHIND THE DIMMER.**
This can be a bit of a trick, as outlet boxes generally come in 1 size—too small.

15 PLACE THE MOUNTING SCREWS, which you hope are still sitting safely in the old switch, **INTO THE MOUNTING STRAPS.** Don't forget the fiber washers. **SCREW THE DIMMER INTO THE BOX.**
This is easier said than done; 1 hand holds the dimmer, 1 hand holds the screw, and who operates the screwdriver? Think about your lovely dinner, and you will immediately find yourself holding and operating 3 things at once.

16 REPLACE THE SWITCH COVER PLATE.
Atmosphere is just around the corner.

17 PLACE THE DIMMER KNOB ON THE KNURLED POST.
It looks wonderful but isn't quite functional—yet.

18 TURN ON THE POWER
and fly back to the new dimmer.

19 TAKE A DEEP BREATH AND PUSH IN THE DIMMER KNOB. KEEP YOUR EYES ON THE CEILING BEACON. AS YOU TURN THE DIMMER KNOB, YOU WILL WATCH THE BLAZE TURN TO A SOFT, WARM GLOW.
Close all the curtains and try it again. You have just created your idea of heaven on earth!

HELPFUL HINT
DIMMER SWITCHES AREN'T JUST FOR CREATING ATMOSPHERE. THEY ARE ALSO GREAT FOR SAVING ENERGY. Better still, use flashlights around the house and leave the lights off altogether.

REPAIRING A LAMP SOCKET OR SWITCH

You know you have to do it when you're reading in bed one night. You get to the best part of the book and the lamp goes out, all by itself. Thinking it must be the fuse, you get out of bed, but the minute your feet hit the floor, the lamp magically goes on. Climb back into bed, and as your head hits the pillow, the lamp goes off. You reach over and fiddle with the switch. "Off" works fine, but "on" happens only after a 10-second delay or a good shake.

1 **RESIST THE TEMPTATION TO THROW THE LAMP IN THE GARBAGE.**
That's impulse destroying. You can fix it. **CHECK TO SEE IF THE CORD IS FRAYED.** If it's intact and you've already checked the bulb and the fuse, you have to replace the socket or switch. Take heart—a new socket is a whole lot cheaper than a new lamp.

2 **UNPLUG THE LAMP AND FIND A NICE, COMFY PLACE TO WORK.**
I like to sit on the living room floor at the coffee table. It's the only debris-free place in the house.

3 **REMOVE THE SHADE AND THE BULB AND SAVE BOTH,**
unless you hate the shade.

4 **IF THE LAMP HAS A *HARP*,** a large metal frame that supports the shade, **REMOVE IT BY SLIDING THE SMALL METAL SLEEVES UP THE ARMS OF THE HARP AND SQUEEZING THE ARMS TOGETHER TO RELEASE IT FROM THE LAMP.**

5 **SOMEWHERE ON THE OUTER SHELL OF THE SOCKET IS STAMPED "PRESS." DO IT AND AT THE SAME TIME PULL OFF THE OUTER SHELL AND THE INSU-LATING SLEEVE INSIDE IT.**
Wouldn't it be lovely if everything came with an instruction printed on it? It would take all the guessing out of fixing. On second thought, why spoil the fun?

6 **ON EACH SIDE OF THE SWITCH IS A TERMINAL SCREW. LOOSEN BOTH SCREWS AND REMOVE THE WIRE FROM EACH TERMINAL TO REMOVE THE SWITCH.**

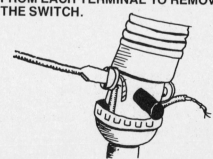

7 CHECK THE CONDITION OF THE SOCKET CAP.
I always thought that caps were on tops, but not this one. It's on the bottom of the socket, facing up. **IF IT'S BENT OR DAMAGED, NOW IS THE TIME TO REPLACE IT.** If it's in good shape, leave it there. You'll save time, steps, and the new socket cap that comes with every new socket.

8 TO REMOVE THE SOCKET CAP, LOOSEN THE SET SCREW ON THE OUTSIDE OF THE CAP BASE.
"Loosen" is sufficient; "remove" the screw, and it's "lost." **STOP. BEFORE YOU UNTIE THE KNOT THAT SHOULD BE SITTING IN THE CAP, DRAW IT** with pencil and paper. It's called an *underwriter's knot*, as in

"insurance," because it keeps the cord from being pulled off the terminals. **GOT YOUR PICTURE? UNTIE THE KNOT AND UN-SCREW THE CAP FROM THE LAMP TUBE,** the metal tube that runs up the center of most lamps. It houses the cord and keeps all the parts organized in a solid, vertical line.

9 THREAD THE CORD THROUGH THE BOTTOM OF THE NEW SOCKET CAP AND SCREW THE SOCKET CAP TO THE LAMP TUBE. TIGHTEN THE SET SCREW, THEN STOP.

10 CHECK THE ENDS OF THE CORD THAT WENT AROUND THE TERMINALS.
If they're frayed, you have to cut them off and strip them; this means a little extra cord. **AND IF YOU'RE TYING A KNOT WHERE THERE WASN'T ONE BEFORE,** you need a little extra cord. **PULL AS MUCH CORD AS YOU THINK YOU'LL NEED THROUGH THE LAMP.** If you don't need the extra cord for either reason, you've just read what you don't need to do.

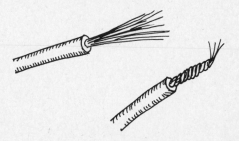

11 REFERRING TO YOUR PICTURE, TIE AN UNDERWRITER'S KNOT IN THE CORD. GET IT AS LOW DOWN IN THE SOCKET CAP AS POSSIBLE.
P.S. If you took the socket apart and didn't see a knot, don't think this means, "Oh good, I don't have to bother." The manufacturer may not have bothered, but it's always nice to have insurance.

12 IF THE WIRES NEED TO BE CUT AND STRIPPED, USE WIRE STRIPPERS.

TWIST EACH SET OF NEWLY EXPOSED STRANDS TOGETHER—not together together but together separately—**ON EACH SIDE OF THE CORD AND WRAP**

ONE AROUND EACH TERMINAL SCREW, CLOCKWISE.
This keeps the strands from heading off in different directions when you tighten the terminal screws. Remember, you don't want a lot of extra cord hanging around. It won't all fit into the socket.

13 TIGHTEN THE TERMINAL SCREWS.

14 CHECK TO SEE THAT THE INSULATING SLEEVE IS STILL INSIDE THE SHELL AND THEN REPLACE THE SHELL BY FIRMLY PRESSING IT INTO THE CAP.

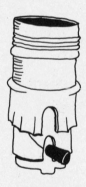

If you got rid of any excess wire, then this will all go together neatly. If you didn't, it probably won't go together at all. Don't get discouraged. Smile. You already know how it's supposed to go. A little fiddling with the wires and you'll have it all organized and operational. To get this right the first time is really sheer luck—honest! Fiddling is almost compulsory.

15 REPLACE THE HARP, THE SHADE, AND THE BULB.

16 THIS IS WHAT YOU'VE BEEN WAITING FOR. TAKE THE LAMP BACK TO YOUR BEDSIDE TABLE AND PLUG IT IN. GET YOUR BOOK AND TURN ON THE LAMP SWITCH. READ AWAY WITH THE LAMP SHINING BRIGHTLY.
Who cares if it's the middle of the day?

HELPFUL HINT
NEVER LEAVE A LAMP PLUGGED IN WITH THE SOCKET EMPTY. ALWAYS REPLACE A LIGHT BULB WITH A NEW ONE IMMEDIATELY. If you don't have a new bulb, put the old one back. The lamp is now a table decoration.

INSTALLING A SMOKE DETECTOR

No house is truly safe without one. They even have them in the fire station!

1 **BUY 1 OR 2 OR 3.**
You can never have too many.

2 **READ THE INSTRUCTIONS THOROUGHLY.**
"Thoroughly" means read them again.

3 **DETERMINE WHERE TO INSTALL THE DETECTOR.**
This is probably the most important step because a smoke detector in the wrong place won't save anyone's life.

SOME "WHERE TO'S":

ON EVERY FLOOR OR LEVEL OF THE HOUSE.
Don't forget the bottom of the basement stairwell.

IN THE CENTER OF EVERY HALLWAY.

AT THE TOP AND BOTTOM OF EVERY STAIRWELL.

IN EVERY SLEEPING AREA.

IN EVERY BEDROOM WHERE SOMEONE SLEEPS WITH THE DOOR CLOSED.

IN EVERY ROOM WHERE A POTENTIAL FIRE HAZARD EXISTS—THE LAUNDRY ROOM, WORKSHOP, ETC.

AS CLOSE TO THE CENTER OF THE CEILING AS POSSIBLE.
Of course, if you put detectors in all these places, you'll end up living in a giant smoke detector. Usually 3 or 4, well placed, are sufficient.

SOME "WHERE NOT TO'S":

IN THE KITCHEN.
Install one at least 20 feet away or the alarm will sound every time you burn the bacon.

IN THE BATHROOM.
Moisture will set off the alarm.

33

NEAR A FORCED-AIR DUCT OR AIR CONDITIONER.

NEAR THE FURNACE.

NEAR A FLUORESCENT LIGHT FIXTURE.

IN THE SPACE WHERE THE WALL MEETS THE CEILING OR AT THE TOP OF AN A-FRAME CEILING.
These are "dead air" spaces, and the dead air prevents the smoke from rising.

IN THE GARAGE.
Dust and stray bugs, to say nothing of spiders, will set it off.

4 **REMOVE THE FACE COVER FROM THE DETECTOR AND INSERT THE BATTERIES.**
Smoke detectors usually come with batteries. Use them. If you don't, the detector won't work, and you're about to go to a lot of trouble for nothing.

5 **HOLD THE DETECTOR,** without the face cover (if you don't, this step won't work), **AGAINST THE CEILING AND MARK THE SCREW HOLES WITH A PENCIL.**
Easier said than done—if you don't hurry, your arms will start to fall off. **IF THE SCREW HOLES LOOK LIKE THIS,**

THEY ARE CALLED *KEYHOLES,* **AND YOU SHOULD OUTLINE THEM AND SKIP STEPS 6 AND 7.** Don't worry, you're not missing anything. You'll get to do all the same stuff in Step 8.

6 **DRILL HOLES FOR THE SCREWS AND INSERT THE PLASTIC ANCHORS.**
Don't leave these out, or the detector could land on someone's head—probably yours.

7 **HOLD THE DETECTOR IN PLACE, AND INSERT AND TIGHTEN THE SCREWS.**
This is where you need 3 hands.

8 **IF THE SCREW HOLES ARE KEYHOLES, DRILL HOLES IN THE SKINNY ENDS OF THE KEYHOLES AND INSERT THE ANCHORS** *WITHOUT* **THE DETECTOR IN PLACE. SCREW IN THE SCREWS** (this is not a misprint) **AND BACK EACH SCREW OFF 2 FULL TURNS.**
Take a breath and reorganize the circulation in your hands and arms. **PLACE THE DETECTOR SO THAT THE LARGE ENDS OF THE KEYHOLES ARE OVER THE SCREWS, AND TURN THE DETECTOR**

SO THAT THE SCREWS "LOCK" INTO THE SMALL KEYHOLE SLOTS. TIGHTEN THE SCREWS. This kind of installation makes it easier to remove the detector for cleaning, to change the batteries, and to take it with you when you move. What you do about the screws left in the ceiling, I'll leave up to you.

ing things. Some time later you'll hear another "beep-beep," and you'll think someone's left something on somewhere. You'll check around—nothing. "Beep-beep." Oh, no, not again. What is it? At some point while you are frantically searching for this thing you keep hearing, or at least think you're hearing, you'll walk right under the smoke detector, and the "beep-beep" will happen. You'll almost have a heart attack, but at the same time you'll be overwhelmed with relief that you're not going deaf, or crazy. In fact, it's the smoke detector telling you to...

12 **CHANGE THE BATTERIES, IMMEDIATELY,** even if it means a trip to the store in the rain or snow or both. **IMMEDIATELY. AND ONLY USE NEW BATTERIES.** Batteries from the kids' electronic games are not reliable, and who needs that "beep-beep" more than once a year?

"beep!" "beep!"

9 **REPLACE THE FACE COVER AND PRESS THE TEST BUTTON FOR A FULL 10 SECONDS.**
You won't like the sound at all. Count to 10, loud. This is a diversionary tactic designed to make you concentrate on something other than the pain in your ears.

10 **PRESS THE TEST BUTTON ONCE A MONTH.**

11 **VACUUM THE DETECTOR ONCE A YEAR AND NEVER NEGLECT IT.**
It won't let you. One day you'll hear a faint "beep-beep"—you'll think you hear it, that is. You'll convince yourself that you're hear-

HELPFUL HINTS
BUY A SMOKE DETECTOR THAT NOT ONLY HAS AN ALARM BUT ALSO HAS AN ESCAPE LIGHT. It's a mini-flashlight, strong enough to show the way out if a fire occurs in the middle of the night.

CHECK WITH THE FIRE DEPARTMENT TO SEE IF IT HAS WINDOW STICKERS FOR BEDROOMS. PUT THEM IN EACH ROOM WHERE A PERSON SLEEPS. IN THE MIDDLE OF THE NIGHT THE FIRE FIGHTERS WILL GO TO THESE ROOMS FIRST.

35

Things you learned and might like to remember for next time.

AND ELIMINATING FLOOR SQUEAKS
Totally unrelated but necessary to keep you both warm and sane.

squeek

MAKING A FIREPLACE PLUG

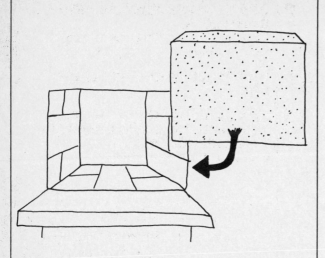

This is the best way to keep heat from going up the chimney when you're not using the fireplace. Don't depend on dampers.

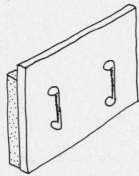

1 MEASURE THE FIREPLACE OPENING EXACTLY.
Write the measurements down, **AND ADD 4″ TO THE WIDTH AND 2″ TO THE HEIGHT.**

2 CUT A PIECE OF 1/2″ PLYWOOD TO THIS SIZE.
If you've made friends with someone at the lumber yard, you can get it cut for you.

3 CUT A PIECE OF STYROFOAM THAT IS 3″ OR 4″ THICK (it's messy no matter how you do it) **TO THE EXACT MEASUREMENTS OF THE FIREPLACE OPENING.**
Remember, you wrote them down—you did,

didn't you? The *exact* part has to do with the snug fit of the styrofoam. A tighter fit means less warm air can escape up the chimney.

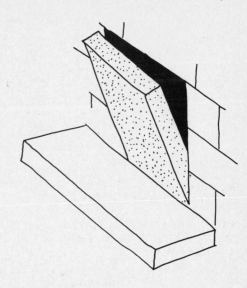

4 **TO THE FACE OF THE PLYWOOD ATTACH 2 HANDLES.**
This choice is creative and yours. Drawer pulls are attractive and work well, and 2 work better than 1 when it comes to pulling the finished plug from the fireplace.

5 PLACE THE PLYWOOD HANDLE-SIDE DOWN. DECIDE WHICH END IS THE BOTTOM—it doesn't matter which—**AND POSITION THE STYROFOAM SO THAT THE BOTTOM OF THE STYROFOAM AND THE BOTTOM OF THE PLYWOOD**

ARE EVEN AND THE STYROFOAM IS CENTERED 2″ FROM EACH SIDE OF THE PLYWOOD.
This matters!

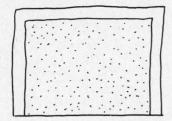

6 **MARK THIS POSITION AND REMOVE THE STYROFOAM PIECE.**

7 **COVER THE SURFACE OF THE STYRO-FOAM LIBERALLY WITH WHITE GLUE OR EPOXY.**

Adhesives like contact cement will melt the styrofoam. **REPLACE IT IN THE MARKED POSITION ON THE PLYWOOD.**

8 **FIRMLY PRESS THE 2 PIECES TO-GETHER AND WEIGHT OR CLAMP THEM TO DRY.**
Encyclopedias are great weights, and if you haven't got a C-clamp, try tying the whole shebang with a pantyhose tourniquet.

9 **REMOVE THE EXCESS GLUE WITH A DAMP CLOTH.**
If you used epoxy, don't make a mess. Oops, too late!

10 **WAIT 24 HOURS FOR THE PLUG TO DRY.**

11 **DECORATE THE FACE OF THE PLUG WITH TILES, WALLPAPER, PAINT, OR WHATEVER YOU LIKE.**
Give your imagination a chance.

12 **PUT THE PLUG INTO THE FIREPLACE WHENEVER IT'S COLD, AND SIT BACK AND ENJOY A TOASTY WARM ROOM.**

Note: This is a really good idea!

13 **REMOVE THE PLUG TO LIGHT A FIRE AND ON CHRISTMAS EVE.**

HELPFUL HINT
USE A HACKSAW BLADE WITH 1 END TAPED TO CUT STYROFOAM.

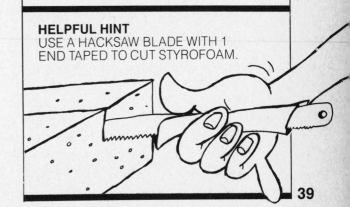

ELIMINATING FLOOR SQUEAKS

There are squeaks and then there are squeaks, squeaks to get rid of and squeaks to be left as they are. The ones that must go are the squeaks that you have learned to navigate around because stepping on those particular places drives you wild. You find that you have various alternate routes around the kitchen, and then one day you catch yourself in mid-step, almost fall headlong into the dinner you're trying to fix, and make the decision to eliminate the squeak before you eliminate yourself. The squeaks that are better left alone are the ones that let you know someone is sneaking downstairs to watch television in the middle of the night. Put eliminating them on your list of things to do in your old age, when all the children have left home.

1 **IF THE SQUEAK IS ON THE MAIN FLOOR, HEAD FOR THE BASEMENT TO LOCATE THE TROUBLE SPOT.** This is a lot easier to do if someone hops on the squeak upstairs. If the dog is your only helper, get him to sit on the spot until you're under where you think it is, and then call him; the squeak will happen as he gets up. If the dog isn't interested, try encouraging him with dog cookies. Zeke will do anything for a cookie.

2 **IF IT APPEARS THAT ONE OF THE FLOORBOARDS (SUBFLOOR) HAS PULLED AWAY FROM THE JOIST, FIND A PIECE OF WOOD TO SERVE AS A WEDGE.** Wood shingles are terrific wedges. **HAMMER THE WEDGE BETWEEN THE FLOORBOARD AND JOIST.**

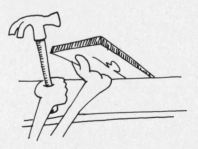

Don't push your luck and push the wedge in so far that you raise the subfloor. All you want to do is keep the board from moving every time it's stepped on.

3 IF MORE THAN ONE OF THE FLOORBOARDS ARE LOOSE AND THE WEDGE ISN'T WIDE ENOUGH TO COVER THEM, BUTT A PIECE OF 1″ x 4″ SCRAP LUMBER UP AGAINST THE FLOORBOARDS. MAINTAIN A STEADY, EVEN PRESSURE ON THE PIECE OF 1″ x 4″ AND NAIL IT TO THE JOIST.

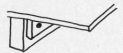

Make sure your helper isn't sitting or standing on the squeaky area. His "help" only keeps the floorboards flush with the joist. Once he gets off the squeak, the boards will rise, the squeak will return, and you won't have eliminated anything.

4 IF IT APPEARS THAT THE JOISTS ARE IMPROPERLY SPACED, BRIDGED, OR ARE WARPED, CUT SOLID BLOCKS OF 2″ LUMBER THAT ARE THE SAME LENGTH AS THE DISTANCE BETWEEN THE JOISTS AND FIT THEM TIGHTLY BETWEEN THE JOISTS.

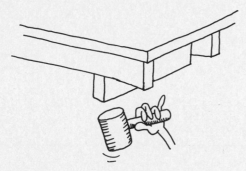

All this is to make more solid that which wants to move around just enough to give you a squeak or two.

5 IF THE SUBFLOOR IS INACCESSIBLE (the squeaks happen on the second floor), FORCE EITHER POWDERED GRAPHITE, TALCUM POWDER, WOOD GLUE, OR TRIANGULAR GLAZIER'S POINTS INTO THE JOINTS BETWEEN THE FLOORBOARDS.
None of these mar the surface of the wood. What you don't need to go with the squeak is a wrecked floor.

6 IF YOU HAVE TRIED ALL OF THE ABOVE AND THE SQUEAK IS STILL SQUEAKING, NAIL THE FLOORBOARD TO THE JOIST FROM ABOVE. DRILL PILOT HOLES—you don't want to split the floorboard—AND COUNTERSINK THE NAIL HEADS.

Countersink means getting the nail heads below the wood surface so that you can cover them with wood filler. It also means getting rid of potential foot killers and a floor with the texture of a porcupine.

7 IF YOU HAVE ELIMINATED THE SQUEAK IN THE KITCHEN FLOOR, GET USED TO WALKING IN DIRECT ROUTES ONCE AGAIN.
This will take some time, but you will enjoy every minute of it!

HELPFUL HINT
MAKE YOUR OWN WOOD FILLER WITH SAWDUST AND WHITE GLUE. If you don't have any sawdust, make some.

41

Things you learned and might like to remember for next time.

PAINTING

*Or trying to get more
on the wall than on you.*

PAINTING HINTS

Read these before you paint. If you don't, you'll wish you had.

1 **TO SELECT A GOOD BRUSH, USE THE BOUNCE TEST.** No, this is not a television commercial. **BOUNCE THE BRUSH ON THE BACK OF YOUR HAND TO TEST FOR SPRING AND ELASTICITY. THEN FAN THE BRISTLES TO SEE IF ANY BRISTLES ARE ABOUT TO FALL OUT. REMOVE LOOSE BRISTLES, BOUNCE, AND FAN AGAIN. IF MORE LOOSE BRISTLES APPEAR, REPLACE THE BRUSH ON THE STORE RACK AND TRY ANOTHER ONE.** If all the bristles fall out, you've just bought it.

2 **BEFORE PAINTING, PUNCH SEVERAL NAIL HOLES AROUND THE RIM OF THE PAINT CAN. THIS RETURNS THE EXCESS PAINT TO THE CAN INSTEAD OF LETTING IT RUN DOWN THE SIDE AND ALL OVER THE FLOOR.**

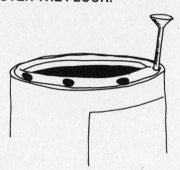

This is an economical hint; think of all the paint you'll save to use on the wall instead of painting the can.

3 **TO MAKE CLEANUP EASY, PUT PETROLEUM JELLY ON YOUR HANDS AND FOREARMS BEFORE YOU START TO PAINT.** Watch it, you still have to hold the brush. A better way to keep paint off you is to play Tom Sawyer: put on the petroleum jelly, then con someone else into painting.

4 **IF YOU HAVE A SHINY, NEW PAINT TRAY OR A YUCKY, RUSTY ONE** and you want to save the tray or keep the rust out of the paint, **PUT THE TRAY INTO A WHITE PLASTIC GARBAGE BAG TO COVER IT.**

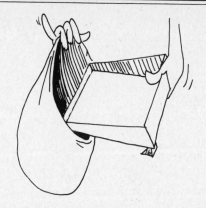

Actually, the color doesn't matter, but you get the idea. **WHEN YOU'RE FINISHED PAINTING, JUST ZIP THE BAG, GOO AND ALL, OFF THE TRAY AND INTO THE GARBAGE. IF YOU'RE OUT OF GARBAGE BAGS, YOU CAN LINE THE TRAY WITH ALUMINUM FOIL.**

5 **PUT A PAPER PLATE UNDER THE PAINT CAN WHILE PAINTING TO KEEP THE INEVITABLE DRIPS FROM LEAVING A PAINT RING ON THE FLOOR EVERY TIME YOU MOVE THE CAN.**

A gooey paint can could become a permanent floor fixture, or you'll keep stepping in the drips and decorate the floors and carpets all over the house.

6 **IF THE PHONE RINGS WHILE YOU'RE PAINTING** and it's your mother-in-law, **PUT THE PAINTBRUSH INTO A PLASTIC BAG AND SEAL IT.** This keeps the brush moist until you've had your free advice for the day.

7 PAINTBRUSHES USED WITH LATEX PAINT CAN BE STORED IN SEALED PLASTIC BAGS IN THE FREEZER FOR SEVERAL WEEKS.

Remember to thaw before using, and if you discover all your paintbrushes are missing, you'll know where to look.

8 TO HELP GET RID OF PAINT ODOR WHILE YOU'RE PAINTING, PUT A SAUCER OF VINEGAR IN THE ROOM OR ADD A FEW DROPS OF VANILLA EXTRACT TO THE PAINT.
Better yet, open the windows. Wear a sweater if it's snowing.

9 WHEN RESEALING THE PAINT CAN, PLACE THE LID ON THE CAN AND COVER IT WITH A CLOTH. NOW WHACK THE LID TIGHT WITH A HAMMER.
The cloth keeps the paint from splattering all over the place.

10 WHEN PAINTING OUTDOORS, INSTEAD OF PICKING BUGS AND DIRT OUT OF THE PAINT WITH YOUR FINGERS, CUT SEVERAL PIECES OF WIRE SCREEN THE DIAMETER OF THE PAINT CAN AND DROP THEM INTO THE CAN PERIODICALLY TO SINK THE DEBRIS.

11 KEEP A RECORD OF THE PAINT COLORS YOU'VE USED ON THE BACK OF A SWITCH COVER PLATE IN THE JUST-PAINTED ROOM.

12 STORE PAINT CANS UPSIDE DOWN TO PREVENT A SKIN FROM FORMING ON THE TOP OF THE PAINT.
Make sure the can is well sealed, or you're in for a surprise the next time you want to use it.

13 BEFORE SEALING THE PAINT CAN, MARK ON THE OUTSIDE THE LEVEL OF THE PAINT IN THE CAN.
It takes the guesswork out of how much is left in there.

14 SAVE LEFTOVER PAINT FOR TOUCH-UPS IN BABY FOOD JARS OR NAIL POLISH BOTTLES.
Just remember where you've stored them, and don't mistake the stored paint for polish.

15 USE PANTYHOSE TO STRAIN LUMPY PAINT.
I have no idea what the lumps could be, but whatever they are, you don't want them on the wall.

Seventy-five percent of the job is getting ready to do it. This is definitely the hard-work part, guaranteed to make you love the painting part.

work better at night, bring in lamps plugged into outlets in other rooms or wear a miner's helmet. If it's the kitchen, work fast or be prepared to cook everything in the freezer.

PREPARATION
Be prepared. This eliminates extra cleanup and many an "Oh darn, I just got paint on my best…"

1 **REMOVE ANYTHING AND EVERYTHING IN THE IMMEDIATE VICINITY THAT YOU HAVE NO INTENTION OF PAINTING.**
If it's too heavy to move or is permanent, like the floor, cover it with a drop cloth. If it moves, get rid of it.

3 **REMOVE WHATEVER HARDWARE YOU CAN—SWITCH AND RECEPTACLE PLATES, DOORKNOBS** (don't close the door), **AND LIGHT FIXTURES.**
If it's forever stuck, mask it with masking tape and/or plastic garbage bags.

2 **TURN OFF THE ELECTRICAL POWER TO THE ROOM.**
You'll cover all the switches and outlets anyway. This is now a daytime job. Or if you

4 **REMOVE OLD WALLPAPER.**
Painting on wallpaper is just asking for trouble. See the section on "Removing Old Wallpaper."

5 **PREPARE THE SURFACE TO BE PAINTED BY SCRAPING, PATCHING, SANDING, AND THOROUGHLY CLEANING EVERY CRACK AND NAIL HOLE.**
Paint is cosmetic, not surgical! Patched areas must be primed.

6 **MASK EVERYTHING IN SIGHT THAT YOU HAVEN'T REMOVED—SWITCH AND OUTLET BOXES, THERMOSTATS, WINDOWPANES, LIGHT FIXTURES, ETC.**

Don't use newspaper to mask because the ink may transfer to that surface. Of course, if you're only painting a table, you can use your own discretion about how far you think the paint will fly.

7 **WASH DOWN THE WALLS** (why not up?) **WITH VINEGAR AND WARM WATER.**
Any residual dust just gums up the paint.

8 **WALLS PAINTED WITH ENAMEL SHOULD BE THOROUGHLY SANDED AND WASHED,**
or the new paint will slide down the wall and run all over the floor.

9 **TAKE A GOOD LOOK AROUND THE ROOM.**
It should look like a bomb hit it! This is your incentive to either get busy and paint or to walk out and close the door.

PAINTING—Finally

Dress for the job ahead, and I don't mean dress up. Wear clothes that are the same color as the paint or cut head and arm holes in a large garbage bag and wear that.

1 **PICK THE COLOR.**
Let everyone in the family in on the discussion and then pick a color to match your earrings.

2 **MAKE FRIENDS WITH YOUR DEALER** (essential) **AND ASK WHAT KIND OF PAINT IS THE BEST FOR WHAT YOU ARE PAINTING AND HOW MUCH YOU'LL NEED.**
If cleanup is a priority and you're already worried about it, use a latex paint; it cleans up with water. Better still, if you're that worried, hire someone to do the job.

3 STIR THE PAINT.
True, they shook it up at the store, but if you've waited a week or more to start, the paint needs a stir because the pigment settles to the bottom of the can. And it requires more than 1 stir around the can.

4 IF YOU'RE PAINTING WITH A LIGHTER COLOR THAN WHAT'S ON THE WALLS, PRIME THE WALLS WITH WHITE PRIMER.
If you're not interested in primer, you're in for 2 coats of paint. Primer is cheaper.

5 ALWAYS START WITH THE CEILING.
You can look at this 2 ways: positively—the worst is over first—or negatively—this is the high-up, overhead part that will make your arms and hands want to fall off. I recommend doing the ceiling while thinking about how easy the walls will be.

6 WITH A GOOD BRUSH, PAINT A HAND-WIDE STRIP ON THE CEILING AROUND THE PERIMETER OF THE ROOM WHERE THE WALLS AND CEILING MEET.
Buy the best brush for the job. If the brush sheds its bristles, you'll spend all your time picking bristles out of what you've just painted and flicking and sticking them everywhere.

7 USING A BRUSH, DIP THE BRISTLES ONLY 1/3 OF THEIR LENGTH INTO THE PAINT, TAP OFF THE EXCESS PAINT, AND APPLY WITH SHORT STROKES. DO NOT USE UNIFORM, SAME-DIRECTION BRUSH STROKES AND ALWAYS WORK FROM A WET, PAINTED AREA OUT TO A DRY, UNPAINTED ONE.
This may help, but remember that the object is to get the paint on the wall, and I'd like to meet the person who painted an entire room without occasionally dunking the brush into the paint right up to the handle.

8 IF THE CEILING IS ALL YOU'RE PAINTING, USE A BRUSH EDGE-ON TO CUT INTO THE CORNERS AND MAKE A STRAIGHT LINE WHERE THE CEILING MEETS THE WALL.
Remember after the first goof that practice makes perfect, and to ensure perfection hang onto a wet rag in your free hand. Of course, if you're holding onto the ladder for dear life, hold the rag in your teeth.

9 USE A ROLLER TO PAINT THE REST OF THE CEILING.
Here 2 things are important. First, buy a good roller. Buy one that accepts an extension handle so you can stand on the floor and paint the ceiling without worrying about a ladder to move or fall off. The roller should also be spiral-wrapped and have a plastic

core. Second, ''speed rolling'' is out. Slow, steady pressure gets the paint evenly on the ceiling; speed rolling gets the paint on you.

10 USING A ROLLER, BEGIN BY MAKING A BROAD M, W, OR X PATTERN, STARTING AT THE BOTTOM OF THE ''LEG.'' EVEN THIS OUT BY MAKING LIGHT STROKES UP AND DOWN, AND FINISH WITH SIDE-TO-SIDE STROKES OVER IT ALL. DO THIS SO AS NOT TO FOLLOW A DEFINITE PATTERN.
Fat chance—after reading these instructions, you couldn't possibly follow any pattern. **ALWAYS WORK FROM A DRY AREA TO ONE THAT HAS BEEN PAINTED.**

11 TAKE A BREAK.
Lie on the floor and look at the ceiling. This will return blood circulation to your arms and hands and give you an overwhelming sense of accomplishment.

✳   ✳   ✳

12 NOW PAINT THE WALLS IN THE SAME MANNER AS THE CEILING. DON'T FORGET TO MAKE THE SAME HAND-WIDE STRIP (Step 5) AROUND WINDOWS, DOOR FRAMES, AND BASEBOARDS.

13 PAINT THE BASEBOARDS, WINDOW TRIM, DOORS, AND DOOR FRAMES IN THIS ORDER.
A cardboard or plastic shield helps when painting trim to keep the paint from running, dripping, and generally going where you don't want it to. If it does, you get to do 2 things at once—clean up and paint.

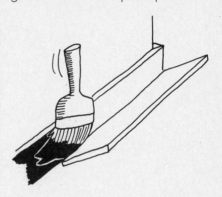

14 MAKE THIS ROOM OUT OF BOUNDS FOR AT LEAST 24 HOURS OR UNTIL THE PAINT IS DRY.
Who needs kids, pets, and grownups adding to or subtracting from your work of art, not to mention the dust or other grot they'll leave behind?

HELPFUL HINT: WET PAINT TEST SIGN
ON A PIECE OF CARDBOARD, MAKE A SIGN THAT SAYS, ''WET PAINT—TEST HERE.'' ADD A GOOD BLOB OF PAINT AND PUT THE SIGN IN A PROMINENT PLACE.

49

Buy a brick house!

This can be a big job because there can be so many problems caused by weather, infrequent painting, inferior paint, and application, but if you're adventurous, then preparation is the key. Prepare all surfaces by scraping, sanding, caulking, sealing, and cleaning. After you've done that, you may be so tired you'll hire someone to paint. Ask your dealer which paints are best for each part of the house, and DON'T START IN THE FALL. PRAY FOR THE WARMEST, DRIEST SUMMER IN 20 YEARS, AND DON'T PAINT ON A WINDY DAY, OR YOUR HOUSE EXTERIOR WILL BE DECORATED '' EARLY BUG.''

How to get the most mileage out of your equipment.

1 **SAY ''IMMEDIATELY'' AND ''THOR-OUGHLY'' 10 TIMES.**
Don't put this job off. If the paint sets on the brushes and rollers, you're asking for a longer, harder job.

2 **CLEAN BRUSHES AND ROLLERS USED WITH LATEX PAINT IN WARM, SOAPY WATER, OR JUST WASH AND RINSE THEM IN WARM WATER.**

3 **SHAKE AND SQUEEZE OUT THE EXCESS WATER.**

4 **COMB THE BRUSH BRISTLES TO STRAIGHTEN THEM.**
Honest, it works. **LAY THE BRUSHES FLAT AND STAND THE ROLLERS ON END TO DRY THOROUGHLY.**

5 **TO STORE, WRAP THE BRUSHES IN HEAVY PAPER OR FOIL.**
Storing a brush without wrapping causes the bristles to eventually fan out, and a fan is impossible to paint with.

6 **BRUSHES AND ROLLERS USED WITH OIL-BASED PAINT** (alkyd is a word you'll run into a lot and may never want to hear again) **MUST BE CLEANED WITH TURPENTINE AND THINNER.**
My advice is to throw away the roller sleeve. Brushes are hard enough to clean, and if you forget Step 1, they become hard, literally—forever, almost.

7 **SOAK THE BRUSHES IN TURPENTINE AND WORK THE BRISTLES ALONG THE BOTTOM AND SIDES OF THE CAN. WEAR GLOVES AND OTHER PROTECTIVE CLOTHING AND SMUSH THE BRISTLES WITH YOUR FINGERS.**
This loosens the paint.

8 **RINSE THE BRUSHES SEVERAL TIMES IN PAINT THINNER**
until they are thoroughly clean. Good luck!

9 **SHAKE OUT THE EXCESS SOLVENT.**
This is best done by shaking the brushes into a plastic bag. I've tried doing this outside, but it's not good for the grass.

10 **WASH THE BRUSHES IN WARM, SOAPY WATER AND RINSE THEM WITH WARM WATER.**
Now try to figure out how to clean the sink.

11 **SHAKE OUT THE EXCESS WATER.**

12 **COMB OUT THE BRISTLES TO STRAIGHTEN THEM.**
A metal comb works best. You could destroy your own comb.

13 **DRY AND STORE THE BRUSHES.**
See Steps 4 and 5.

Note: If you read this before you did it, you may have decided to throw away the brushes as well as the roller sleeves. If you didn't, you may swear off oil-based paint forever and not only throw away the brushes but also throw in the towel.

51

RESTORING DEAD BRUSHES

You forgot to say "immediately" and "thoroughly" 10 times when you finished painting!

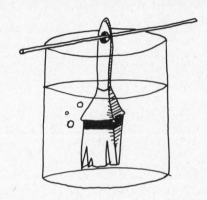

1 **SOAK THE BRUSHES IN A CAN HALF FILLED WITH A COMMERCIAL SOFTENER** (depending on how dead the brushes are, you could try hot vinegar) **BY SUSPENDING THEM FROM WIRE RODS (PIECES OF COAT HANGER) INSERTED THROUGH HOLES DRILLED IN THE HANDLES.**
Don't let the bristles sit on the bottom of the can, or they will become permanently bent, and don't let the softener evaporate, or you'll have dead brushes stuck in a dead can. If this happens, give them all a decent burial. R.I.P.

2 **LET THE BRUSHES SOAK UNTIL THE PAINT IS SOFT.**
This may take a while, so don't hang around to watch.

3 **SCRAPE OFF THE CAKED SURFACE PAINT WITH A PUTTY KNIFE.**
Be careful not to chop off any bristles, or you'll end up with a small broom.

4 SCRAPE PAINT OFF THE INNER BRIS-
TLES WITH THE DULL SIDE OF A DULL
KITCHEN KNIFE.
A sharp kitchen knife is only wishful thinking!

5 COMB OUT THE BRISTLES WITH A
METAL COMB AND SOAK THE BRUSHES
OVERNIGHT.

6 WHEN YOU WAKE UP, IF THERE'S STILL
SOME PAINT IN THE BRISTLES, WASH
THE BRUSHES IN WARM, SOAPY WATER
WITH A LITTLE TURPENTINE ADDED
TO IT.

7 RINSE THE BRUSHES IN CLEAR WATER,
DRY THOROUGHLY, AND WRAP FOR
STORAGE.
All this is guaranteed to make you remember
to say ''immediately'' and ''thoroughly'' 10
times the next time you finish painting!

HELPFUL HINT
PLACE DEAD PAINTBRUSHES IN A
POT OF VINEGAR ON THE STOVE
AND BRING TO A BOIL. SIMMER TO
LOOSEN DRIED PAINT. ADD MORE
VINEGAR IF NECESSARY.

When you want to keep the outside outside and the inside inside.

55

REPLACING A WINDOW PANE

You know you have to do it when you either hear the crash and see the projectile on its flight path or are sitting at the table one night and Babe Ruth Jr. shyly asks you if you've noticed anything different. There is a definite wind blowing around your ankles, and you were just about to ask someone to close the door. ''Yes,'' you say, ''it's windy in here.'' At this point he explains that maybe, somehow, a hole just happened to get in the window. He leads you to the window, and you thank him for letting you know. You also suggest that next time he might tell you when it's still daylight. Now all you can do is vacuum up the broken glass, cover the hole with cardboard and tape, put on a jacket, and hope that the rain forecast for the next day is a mistake.

REPLACING GLASS IN A WOODEN FRAME

1 TAPE NEWSPAPER TO THE INSIDE OF THE WINDOW TO CATCH THE GLASS FRAGMENTS
or leave your piece of cardboard from the night before in place. Notice that it's not raining; with the weather report on your side, today may be your lucky day.

2 PUT ON YOUR HEAVY WORK GLOVES AND YOUR SAFETY GLASSES. HIKE OUTSIDE.
The sun is shining. Wonder what kind of weather they're having at the weather office? **CAREFULLY REMOVE ALL THE LOOSE PIECES OF GLASS FROM THE FRAME.**

3 REMOVE ALL THE OLD PUTTY OR GLAZING COMPOUND FROM AROUND THE FRAME WITH A PUTTY KNIFE OR CHISEL.
Be careful not to gouge the frame. If the dried putty is stubborn and would rather not leave the frame, brush it with linseed oil and let it soak for half an hour to soften it, or use a soldering iron or torch to heat it. Just be careful not to burn the frame—or the house.

4 REMOVE THE GLAZIER'S POINTS, the tiny metal triangles that secure the glass to the frame, **WITH NEEDLE-NOSE PLIERS,** the pliers that are great for getting small things out of tight spaces.

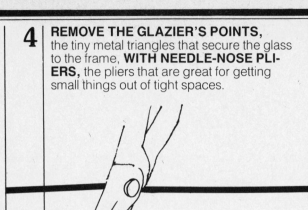

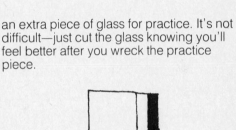

an extra piece of glass for practice. It's not difficult—just cut the glass knowing you'll feel better after you wreck the practice piece.

5 CLEAN THE FRAME SURFACE WITH A WIRE BRUSH AND SAND ALL 4 SIDES OF THE CHANNEL SMOOTH.

6 BRUSH A COAT OF LINSEED OIL AROUND THE CHANNEL. This helps prevent the wood from soaking up the oil in the new putty. Without oil, the putty not only becomes brittle and loses its grip on the window, but it also no longer makes a seal around the glass. In other words, you end up with rattling windows and rotten frames.

7 WITH A GLASS CUTTER AND METAL STRAIGHT EDGE, CUT A NEW PANE OF GLASS 1/8″ SMALLER THAN THE FRAME ON ALL SIDES to allow for irregularities in the frame and for expansion. If you're not interested in learning to use a glass cutter, you could ask someone at the store to cut it for you. If you're determined to cut the glass yourself, see the section, ''Cutting a Piece of Glass,'' and buy

8 WITH A PUTTY KNIFE, APPLY A THIN BED OF GLAZING COMPOUND OR PUTTY ALONG ALL 4 SIDES OF THE FRAME TO MAKE A CUSHION FOR THE GLASS AGAINST STRESS AND LEAKAGE. Of course, it does nothing for *your* stress; it suddenly looks like rain!

9 PRESS THE GLASS FIRMLY INTO PLACE AND REMOVE ANY EXCESS COMPOUND THAT OOZES OUT FROM UNDER THE EDGES OF THE GLASS.

10 Now the fun part. **FASTEN THE GLASS FIRMLY INTO PLACE WITH GLAZIER'S POINTS.**
Glazier's points have no redeeming qualities. They are small, too small for fat fingers. They are also pointy and tend to shoot and drop all over the place. I have tried pushing them into the frame with a putty knife—I gouged the frame. I have tried holding them with needle-nose pliers and pushing them in. I have stood on a ladder and pushed for all I was worth—I pushed myself right off the ladder. I have tried to hold them down with a screwdriver and hit the screwdriver with a hammer—I missed the screwdriver and smashed the glass. In short, get them into the frame any way you can, **USING 2 POINTS ON EACH EDGE OF THE FRAME IF IT IS LESS THAN 10″ SQUARE. IF THE FRAME IS LARGER, USE 1 POINT EVERY 4″. YOU ONLY HAVE TO GET THEM IN HALF WAY, AND SMILE—A LOT!**

11 **FORM THE GLAZING COMPOUND INTO A ROPE 3/8″ IN DIAMETER.**
I put the 3/8″ part in to give you an idea. If you're like me, this part of any instruction is totally meaningless. **PRESS THE STRIPS INTO THE GROOVE ALONG THE EDGES**

OF THE GLASS. It's not going to rain. It's just a little dark.

12 **HOLD A PUTTY KNIFE AT AN ANGLE AND DRAW IT OVER THE COMPOUND TO MAKE A NEAT, TRIANGULAR SEAL.**
Occasionally dip the putty knife in water to keep the compound from sticking to the knife and rolling up in little balls as you draw the knife along its surface. The compound must touch both the glass and the edge of the frame. If you have any doubts, take a look at another window pane to see how someone else did it. That was *not* a raindrop!

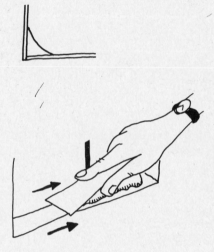

13 **LET THE COMPOUND HARDEN FOR 5 TO 7 DAYS BEFORE PAINTING IT.**
It's raining—find a piece of plastic to cover the window. Smile. You finished replacing the window and tomorrow the sun will shine—the weather forecast said it would!

REPLACING GLASS IN A METAL FRAME

This may not be as messy as working with glazing compound, but it still requires a certain amount of patience. Working with glass goes hand in hand with holding your breath a few times until the glass is securely in the frame. Unfortunately, all metal frames are not the same—that would be too easy. Of course, what you have in your hand seldom, if ever, resembles the illustration in the book. I hope you find the one you have here, but if you're looking at a different species, remember that the person at the store is a wonderful friend.

1 **PUT ON A PAIR OF HEAVY WORK GLOVES AND SAFETY GLASSES.**
You already have a broken window—other complications you don't need, like bandages or trips to the hospital.

2 **CAREFULLY REMOVE ANY PIECES OF BROKEN GLASS THAT MIGHT FALL OUT BEFORE YOU GET STARTED.**
If the glass seems secure in the frame, you don't have to try to remove it yet.

3 **IF THE FRAME RUNS IN A GUIDETRACK AND CAN BE REMOVED, REMOVE IT.**
Removing broken glass from a lying-down window is a lot easier and safer than removing glass from one that is standing up.

4 **LOOK AT THE FRAME TO SEE HOW THE GLASS IS HELD IN PLACE—**
or how what's left of the glass is held in place. **IF THE FRAME IS FASTENED AT THE CORNERS WITH SCREWS THAT GO THROUGH THE MITERED CORNERS LIKE THIS**

you have just found the solution for the broken window. If not, you get to read a little farther. Or you can read this and find out how to repair someone else's window. Read the entire section and you'll be able to repair everyone's windows and maybe make a little money on the side.

• REMOVE THE TOP AND BOTTOM SCREWS OF 1 SIDE AND PULL THE

59

SIDE PIECE FROM THE REST OF THE FRAME.

• **REMOVE ALL THE BROKEN GLASS FROM THE FRAME.**

• **BRUSH THE CHANNEL WITH A WIRE BRUSH TO REMOVE ANY GLASS SHARDS.**
Shards is a great Scrabble word!

• **IN THE METAL CHANNELS ARE RUBBER GASKETS. REMOVE THEM AND FIT**

THEM ONTO THE EDGES OF THE NEW PANE OF GLASS, WHICH SHOULD BE CUT 1/32″ SMALLER THAN THE FRAME ON ALL SIDES.
Unless you're a whiz with a tape measure, this could be a cutting job for the person at the store.

• **SLIDE THE PANE INTO THE FRAME AND REFASTEN THE SIDE PIECE.**
All this could be a little tricky. Just remember to go slowly, be patient, and resist the temptation to take off your gloves.

5 **IF THE PANE IS HELD IN PLACE BY A RUBBER GASKET THAT MUST BE PULLED OUT FROM UNDER A RETAINING LIP ON THE FRAME, LIKE THIS,**

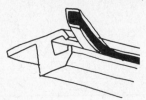

THIS STEP IS FOR YOU.

• Got your gloves on? **LAY THE WINDOW ON A FLAT SURFACE AND REMOVE THE GASKET BY PULLING IT OUT FROM UNDER THE RETAINING LIP.**

• **REMOVE THE BROKEN GLASS FROM THE FRAME AND BRUSH THE CHANNEL CLEAN WITH A WIRE BRUSH.**

• **HAVE THE NEW PANE CUT 1/32″ SMALLER THAN THE FRAME ON ALL SIDES.**
Take the frame to the store if you're worried about measuring in 32nds.

• **CAREFULLY LAY THE NEW PANE IN THE FRAME.**

• **STARTING IN A CORNER, REPLACE THE GASKET BY PRESSING IT UNDER THE RETAINING LIP WITH YOUR THUMB.**
This could take a bit of time, so don't be in a hurry. Resist the temptation to give up. Be careful—you don't want to put your thumb through the glass. And you certainly don't want bandages or any trips to the hospital!

HELPFUL ALUMINUM WINDOW FRAME HINTS
TO KEEP ALUMINUM WINDOW FRAMES IN GOOD CONDITION, REMOVE THE WINDOWS AND CLEAN THE TRACKS. APPLY EITHER PARAFFIN, PASTE WAX, OR SILICONE TO THE METAL SURFACES.

IF THE FRAMES SHOW SIGNS OF OXIDATION, CLEAN THEM WITH STEEL WOOL AND SEAL THEM WITH AUTOMOBILE PASTE WAX.
This should keep them in good condition for at least a year.

CUTTING A PIECE OF GLASS

Removing the pain from making a new pane (I just had to say that) by buying a practice piece of glass.

1 PUT ON A PAIR OF HEAVY WORK GLOVES AND WEAR YOUR SAFETY GLASSES.

2 LAY THE GLASS ON A PADDED SURFACE, LIKE A PIECE OF OLD CARPET OR THIN RUBBER FOAM.

3 BRUSH LINSEED OIL OR TURPENTINE ALONG THE LINE TO BE SCORED AND PLACE A METAL STRAIGHT EDGE ALONG THE CUT MARK.

4 Here it comes. **HOLD THE GLASS CUTTER BETWEEN YOUR FIRST AND SECOND FINGERS**—how I first held a pencil. **SLANT THE CUTTER TOWARD YOU AND PULL IT ALONG THE STRAIGHT EDGE, STARTING ABOUT 1/16″ FROM THE EDGE OF THE GLASS, TO SCORE THE GLASS IN *1 SMOOTH MOTION.*** Do not go back and score it again just in case you think that twice will make it better. Twice is once too many, and you will wreck the edge of the glass.

5 TO DEEPEN THE SCORE, TILT THE GLASS ON ITS EDGE. USING THE BALL AT THE END OF THE CUTTER, LIGHTLY TAP THE GLASS ALONG THE UNDERSIDE OF THE SCORE LINE.

6 PUT A THIN ROD OR DOWEL, AT LEAST AS LONG AS THE SCORE LINE, ON THE WORK SURFACE AND PLACE THE SCORE LINE ON THE GLASS DIRECTLY OVER THE ROD. TAKE A BIG BREATH AND COUNT TO 3. PRESS DOWN FIRMLY ON EITHER SIDE OF THE GLASS.

If the glass snaps clean, you will be overcome with a wonderful sense of accomplishment. If it doesn't, you'll be relieved that it was only your practice piece. Practice on it again before you tackle the good piece.

7 USE AN EMERY STONE OR SILICON CARBIDE SANDPAPER TO SMOOTH THE EDGE, IF NECESSARY.

HELPFUL HINT
FOR SPARKLING CLEAN WINDOWS, WASH THEM WITH A SOLUTION OF VINEGAR AND WATER, AND WIPE THEM CLEAN WITH NEWSPAPER.

REPLACING A SCREEN IN A WOODEN FRAME

This is something I once thought I could do in my free time, somewhere between the laundry, the dishes, the vacuuming, the cooking, the car pooling, the shopping…where is the ''free'' part? If ''free time'' is really the breath you take between jobs, make this a scheduled event.

1 **USING A PUTTY KNIFE, REMOVE THE MOLDING THAT GOES AROUND THE SCREEN FRAME. BE CAREFUL: IF THE MOLDING COMES OFF IN 1 PIECE, YOU CAN REUSE IT.**
It's already measured and cut and it fits, so who wants to go through all this if someone else has done it for you?

2 **REMOVE THE STAPLES OR TACKS THAT HOLD THE SCREEN,** or what's left of it, **TO THE FRAME.**

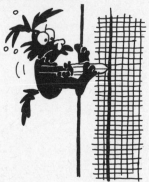

Leave any old staples or tacks in the frame, and they will invariably appear in precisely the spot where you need to put a new one. It could also mean that the molding will never again be snug with the frame.

3 **REMOVE THE SCREEN BUT DON'T THROW IT AWAY.**
If it's in 1 piece, it will make a terrific pattern. If it's in several pieces, they, too, will come in handy someday—remnants are like that. Roll them up and put them in the junk drawer along with all the other good stuff that'll come in handy someday.

4 If your pattern looks more like a mesh bikini, **MEASURE THE OUTSIDE OF THE SCREEN FRAME AND CUT THE NEW SCREENING TO THAT MEASUREMENT.** If you're using nylon or fiberglass screening, make sure you have enough screening to make the 3/4″ hem described in Step 5.

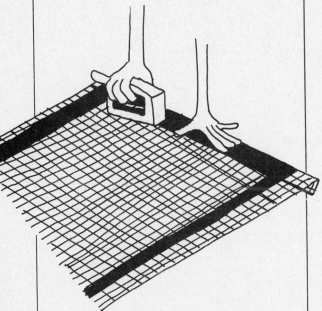

5 **STAPLE OR TACK 1 EDGE OF THE SCREENING TO THE FRAME. IF YOU'RE WORKING WITH NYLON OR FIBER-GLASS SCREENING, FOLD THE EDGES TO MAKE A 3/4″ HEM BEFORE YOU TACK.** Stapling or tacking through the hem reduces the possibility of tearing the material so you won't end up making exactly what you're trying to replace.

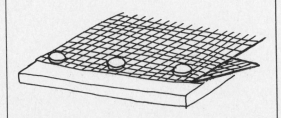

6 **FASTEN EACH SIDE BY PULLING THE SCREENING TIGHT AS YOU GO AND WORK FROM THE CENTER OF EACH SIDE TO THE CORNERS.** Always do the side opposite your first edge last.

7 **TRIM OFF THE EXCESS SCREENING WITH SCISSORS OR A UTILITY KNIFE.** Be careful not to cut the newly installed screen or you'll have to go back to Step 2, and you won't like yourself a lot!

8 **REPLACE THE MOLDING WITH FINISH-ING NAILS AND COUNTERSINK THE NAIL HEADS WITH A NAIL SET.** This means poking the nailheads below the molding surface.

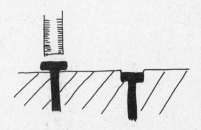

9 **FILL ALL THE HOLES AND COVER ALL THE NAIL HEADS WITH WOOD FILLER.**

10 **PRIME AND REPAINT THE FRAME.** If it's July and it feels like the hottest day of the summer, put the screen up and worry about appearances later. There's a lot to be said for being cool and bug-free.

HELPFUL HINT
KEEP WOODEN FRAMES PAINTED TO PREVENT ROT, MOISTURE AB-SORPTION, AND SWELLING. DON'T STORE SCREENS OVER THE WINTER ON THE WINDOWS. Try a nice, dry indoor place—they last a whole lot longer—maybe under your bed.

REPLACING A SCREEN IN A METAL FRAME

1 **REMOVE THE OLD PIECE OF SCREEN BY REMOVING THE SPLINE FROM ITS CHANNEL.**
Spline may be your new word for the day; it's the skinny, rubbery, tubular stuff that runs around the screen frame and holds the screen in place. The person at the store will know exactly what you're talking about; if not, you can teach them a new word. **DON'T THROW EITHER AWAY.** You can use them as patterns to show the person at the store if you have no confidence in your ability to measure.

2 If you're good at measuring, **MEASURE THE OUTSIDE DIMENSIONS OF THE FRAME FOR THE NEW SCREENING AND THE NEW SPLINE.**
Don't reuse the old spline if it is brittle or broken. Always start with new; old almost always falls apart, and you'll have to make another trip to the store.

3 **BUY NEW SCREENING AND SPLINE.**
Nylon or fiberglass screening is easier to work with than metal. Spline comes in varying degrees of skinny and fat; ask at the store. Better yet, take a piece of the old spline with you. **AND BUY A SPLINE**

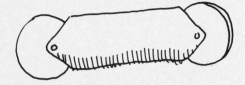

ROLLER—you'll be glad you did. If you decide not to buy one, you get to improvise Steps 5 and 6.

4 **CUT THE SCREENING TO THE OUTSIDE DIMENSIONS OF THE FRAME AND PLACE IT OVER THE FRAME.**
It helps to put several pieces of scrap lumber or a couple of books under the material to keep it somewhat level while you work. **IF YOUR REPLACEMENT SCREENING IS NYLON OR FIBERGLASS, SKIP STEPS 5 AND 6. YOURS IS STEP 7.** Metal is more difficult than nylon—2 steps to 1.

5 **IF THE REPLACEMENT SCREENING IS METAL, CREASE IT INTO THE SPLINE CHANNEL WITH THE CONVEX WHEEL** (the opposite of concave—that helps a lot, doesn't it?—the rounded edge of the wheel that curves out, not in) **OF THE SPLINE**

ROLLER BY STARTING AT THE CORNER ON THE SHORT SIDE OF THE FRAME AND WORKING WITH SHORT BACK-AND-FORTH STROKES.
If the sides of the frame are all the same, you get to designate Side 1.

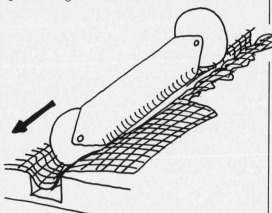

6 **WITH THE CONCAVE WHEEL ON THE ROLLER** (if you figured out convex, concave is on the other end), **FORCE THE SPLINE INTO THE CHANNEL OVER THE SCREENING. BUTT THE CORNER JOINTS AND TAP DOWN THE ENDS CAREFULLY WITH A SCREWDRIVER.**
Poke a hole in the screen and you get to go back to Step 1.

7 **IF THE REPLACEMENT SCREENING IS FIBERGLASS OR NYLON, ROLL THE SPLINE OVER THE SCREENING AND INTO THE FRAME CHANNEL WITH THE CONCAVE** (the rounded edge of the wheel that goes in, as in "in a cave") **WHEEL OF THE SPLINE ROLLER. START IN THE CORNER ON ONE OF THE SHORT SIDES OF THE FRAME AND WORK THE SPLINE INTO THE CHANNEL.**
This may take a bit of back and forth and pressing down.

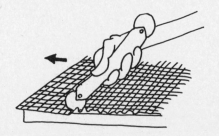

8 DO 1 SHORT SIDE (unless the frame is square) **OF THE FRAME FIRST AND THEN THE 2 LONG SIDES; FINALLY, PULL THE SCREENING TAUT OVER THE END OF THE FRAME OPPOSITE THE FIRST SIDE.**
In other words, it goes: short, long, long, short. Of course, if you don't have shorts and longs, you have to decide tops and bottoms. Always do the side opposite the first side last—honest!

9 **WITH A UTILITY KNIFE, TRIM OFF THE EXCESS SCREENING ALONG THE OUTSIDE EDGE OF THE SPLINE CHANNEL.**
Be careful not to cut on an angle toward the newly installed screen; otherwise, you'll be back at Step 1, and all your smiles will have gone out the window.

MINOR SCREEN REPAIRS

When a tiny tear doesn't require major replacement, this may be a "free time" job, one you do while you drink your coffee, read your mail, and take phone-in advice from your mother-in-law.

METAL SCREEN DIVOTS

1 **TINY HOLES MAY BE FIXED BY POKING THE WIRES BACK INTO PLACE WITH AN AWL. COVER THESE TEARS WITH WATERPROOF GLUE OR CAULK. CLEAR NAIL POLISH MIGHT ALSO DO THE TRICK.**

2 **MAKE A PATCH BY CUTTING A PIECE OF SCRAP SCREENING AND BENDING THE FREE WIRES OF THE PATCH DOWNWARD. PUSH THE WIRES THROUGH THE MESH AROUND THE HOLE AND BEND THE WIRES BACK OVER THE SCREEN TO HOLD THE PATCH IN PLACE.**

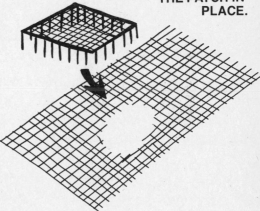

3 **MEND SMALL TEARS BY WEAVING OR DARNING OVER AND AROUND THE RIP WITH STRANDS OF LEFTOVER SCREEN WIRE.**

NYLON OR FIBERGLASS RENTS
A great Scrabble word for *tears*.

1 **CUT A PATCH THAT COVERS THE HOLE.**

2 **GET OUT YOUR IRON AND SET IT ON "WOOL."**
Hot is what you're looking for.

3 **PLACE THE PATCH ON THE SCREEN AND COVER IT WITH A COTTON CLOTH.**
An old dish towel or diaper will do it.

4 **IRON AWAY.**
The heat fuses the patch to the screen.

ALTERING AND INSTALLING

A WINDOW SHADE OR ROLLER BLIND

How to keep from showing the neighbors more than you want to show them.

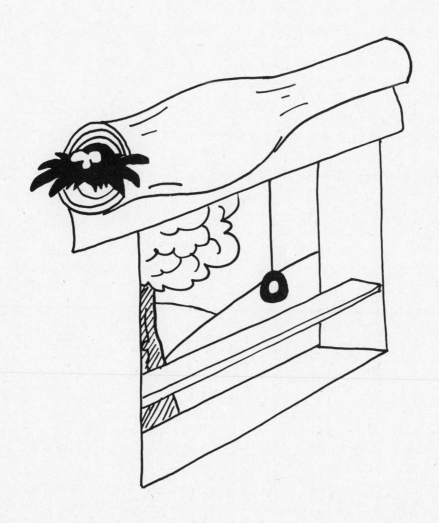

You move into a new house. The first night, dead tired, you climb into the sleeping bag on the floor. Just as you get the bag organized, the streetlight shines through the window and hits you right between the eyes. You try to sleep. Wonder if the town leaves the lights on all night? At 6:00 A.M. the sun is shining brightly through the bare window, the sleeping bag is over your head, and the town turns the lights off at 6:00 A.M. when the sun comes up. Bleary-eyed, you rummage around and find the box marked "window stuff." Open it and there they are, window shades—all too wide for the window. You don't care what you unpack as long as it's your tool box and a saw. There are mounting brackets in the tool box. You hole up in the bedroom and let the rest of the family unpack.

1 ATTACH THE MOUNTING BRACKETS WITH SCREWS TO EITHER THE INSIDE OR OUTSIDE OF THE WINDOW CASING. After a few good, hearty tugs on the shade, nails can work loose and eventually "tug" out. As you face the window, **THE BRACKET WITH THE HANGER SLOT MUST GO ON THE LEFT** (your left, not that of your neighbor who is watching on the

other side of the window). **THE BRACKET WITH THE HOLE IN ITS CENTER MUST GO ON THE RIGHT SIDE OF THE WINDOW.**
There are flush mounting brackets available for the inside of the window casing, but other brackets must extend out from the window frame at a 90° angle. If you mount the brackets on the outside of the casing, just measure each side accurately so that you won't end up with a shade that heads down-

hill. Make sure that a shade mounted on the inside of the casing will clear the top of the casing when it's rolled up; otherwise, rolled up, it will be stuck and decorative as opposed to free-rolling and functional.

4 **REMOVE THE WOODEN SLAT FROM THE HEM OF THE SHADE.** You'll see why in a step or two.

5 **TAKE A GOOD LOOK AT THE WOODEN ROLLER IN YOUR HAND.** A round metal pin pokes out of 1 end, and a flat metal piece, called a *flat pin*, pokes out of the other end. The end with the round pin in it is the one you want to saw off. This is a "look before you leap" step: saw off the wrong end, and you can kiss the shade and your good night's sleep goodbye!

2 **TO MOUNT THE WINDOW SHADE ON THE INSIDE OF THE CASING, MEASURE THE WIDTH BETWEEN THE MOLDINGS AND SUBTRACT 1/8″.** This is to allow for play in the roller; without play, it will be smushed and won't be free to roll anywhere. **TO MOUNT THE SHADE ON THE OUTSIDE OF THE CASING, MEASURE THE WIDTH BETWEEN THE 2 INSTALLED BRACKETS.** In either case, write it down. You're tired!

3 **UNROLL THE SHADE AND REMOVE IT FROM THE ROLLER BY REMOVING ANY STAPLES OR TACKS THAT ARE HOLDING IT IN PLACE.** At this point you might contemplate tacking up the material for the time being. Don't. One day you'll forget that it isn't really a shade and try to roll it up.

6 **BY MEASURING FROM THE FLAT PIN END TO THE ROUND PIN END OF THE ROLLER, MARK YOUR STEP 2 MEASUREMENT ON THE ROUND PIN END OF THE ROLLER.** If I seem to be overstating my case about which end to cut off, it's only because I have my own little supply of roller shades that I turned into dowels. **CUT OFF THE EXCESS WITH A SAW.** Don't throw this piece away or you'll have to fish it out of the garbage.

7 **PULL THE PIN STRAIGHT OUT OF THE BARREL OF THE EXCESS PIECE WITH A PAIR OF PLIERS AND REMOVE THE BARREL ANY WAY YOU CAN.**

You could use a screwdriver to slowly pry the barrel off the end. Be careful not to destroy the edges of the barrel or poke yourself with the screwdriver. They should make special tools for these odd jobs.

69

8 PUT THE BARREL ON THE NEWLY CUT END OF THE ROLLER.
Maybe there *is* a special tool. Maybe the person at the store...

9 HAMMER THE PIN INTO THE ROLLER STRAIGHT THROUGH THE HOLE IN THE BARREL.
Put something under the other end as you hammer or you'll put a ding in your floor or a hole in your carpet.

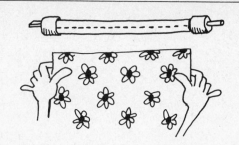

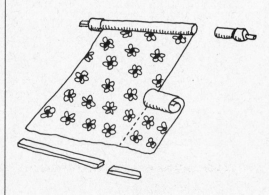

10 TO MAKE THE SHADE MATERIAL THE SAME WIDTH AS THE ROLLER, MEASURE ONLY THE WOODEN SECTION OF THE ROLLER. MARK THIS MEASUREMENT AT SEVERAL POINTS DOWN THE LENGTH OF THE MATERIAL.

11 DRAW A LINE TO JOIN THESE MARKS AND CAREFULLY CUT THE MATERIAL WITH EITHER SCISSORS OR A METAL STRAIGHT EDGE AND UTILITY KNIFE.
Use whatever is in your tool box. You don't need to unpack any more boxes when you're finally hot on the trail of a good night's sleep.

12 POSITION THE END OF THE SHADE MATERIAL ALONG THE GUIDELINE STAMPED ON THE ROLLER.
Make sure the material covers only the wood and not the metal ends of the roller. EITHER STAPLE OR TACK THE SHADE TO THE ROLLER. Staples are easier; with tacks, a hammer, the shade material, and the round surface of the roller before you, you won't know what to hit first. It'll probably be your finger and thumb that are trying to hold the baby tack in place on the round surface that is trying to shoot away from you. Space the staples or tacks evenly; otherwise, the shade will wind off-center.

13 CUT THE HEM SLAT TO FIT THE NEW HEM.

14 REPLACE THE HEM SLAT.
Resist the temptation to use it as a paint stirrer. It keeps the corners of the shade from eventually curling up.

15 ROLL UP THE SHADE AND PUT IT INTO THE BRACKETS.

16 PULL DOWN THE SHADE.
Lovely, it's dark. Crawl into your sleeping bag; no one will miss you for a while. You can worry about the fact that the shade doesn't go up and adjust the tension when you've had a little more sleep—to adjust *your* tension.

ADJUSTING THE TENSION OF A WINDOW SHADE OR ROLLER BLIND

When what rolls down stays down, and when what rolls up flies out of your hand before you have any kind of grip on the shade.

1 **IF THE SPRING TENSION IS TOO GREAT,** the shade positively zings to the top of the window. **TAKE THE ROLLER OUT OF THE BRACKETS AND UNROLL 6″ TO 8″ OF MATERIAL. PUT THE ROLLER BACK INTO THE BRACKETS AND WORK THE SHADE UP AND DOWN A FEW TIMES TO ESTABLISH THE TENSION.** If it still winds up too quickly, repeat this step.

2 **IF THE SPRING TENSION IS TOO LOOSE,** the pulled-down shade doesn't want to go back up. Maybe it's tired. **PULL THE SHADE ABOUT HALFWAY DOWN AND LET THE RATCHET CATCH. REMOVE THE ROLLER FROM THE BRACKETS AND ROLL ABOUT 6″ TO 8″ OF THE SHADE ONTO THE ROLLER. REPLACE THE ROLLER IN THE BRACKETS AND WORK THE SHADE UP AND DOWN TO ESTABLISH THE TENSION.** Repeat this if necessary until the shade rolls up smoothly and evenly.

HELPFUL HINTS
YOU CAN MAKE INSULATED WINDOW SHADES BY REPLACING THE SHADE MATERIAL WITH INSULATED DRAPERY MATERIAL.

IF YOU MAKE A FABRIC SHADE THAT WILL NEED WASHING OR CLEANING, GLUE A STRIP OF VELCRO ONTO THE WOODEN ROLLER WITH CONTACT CEMENT AND SEW THE OTHER VELCRO STRIP TO THE TOP EDGE OF THE FABRIC. This makes removing the fabric a real snap—or should I say a real zip—whatever sound undoing Velcro makes.

Things you learned and might like to remember for next time.

PLUMBING

It breaks down only on weekends, holidays, or in the middle of the night!

REMOVING A SINK TRAP TO CLEAR CLOGS OR RETRIEVE LOST OBJECTS

It's more often than not retrieving somebody's best something, or marbles or toothbrushes or grapes or . . .

2 PUT AN EMPTY BUCKET UNDER THE TRAP.
There is guaranteed water in this bent piece of pipe.

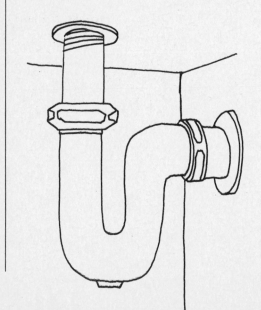

1 ANSWER THE QUESTION, "WHAT IS A TRAP?"
It's the curved piece of plumbing under the sink you've looked at a thousand times and didn't know had a special name. It's sometimes called a P trap. I can't imagine why; it looks nothing at all like a "P." It's there to trap water to make a seal to keep gases from returning to the house, and it often traps objects. You'll be glad it's there when it catches your wedding ring before it shoots off into oblivion.

3 WITH A WRENCH OPEN THE CLEAN-OUT PLUG, IF THERE IS ONE, AT THE BOTTOM OF THE TRAP TO DRAIN IT.
Through this hole you could reach into the trap with a bent wire to clean it out, but of course, there may not be a clean-out plug, and then it's on to the next step.

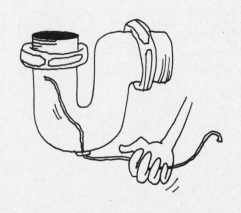

74

4 **GET A PIPE WRENCH,**
also called a monkey wrench. (Why? I don't
know. Maybe it's named for the monkey
using it. Anyway, it's a giant wrench.) If you
don't have one, ask a neighbor; someone
will have one you can borrow. You're not the
only person who ever dropped something
down the drain. **WITH THE WRENCH
JAWS TAPED, UNSCREW THE COUPLING
NUTS THAT ATTACH THE TRAP
TO THE DRAINPIPE AND THE TAIL-
PIECE.** The tailpiece is the piece of pipe that
hightails it up to the sink.

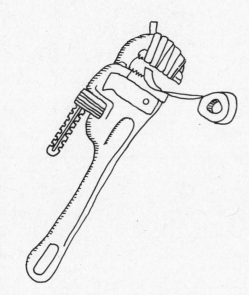

5 **PUSH THE NUTS AND WASHERS ONTO
THE DRAINPIPE AND TAILPIECE.**
You don't want to lose something else.

6 **CROSS YOUR FINGERS AND HOPE
THAT AS YOU TURN THE TRAP OVER
INTO THE BUCKET, THE LOST WHAT-
EVER WILL APPEAR.**
If what you have dropped down the drain is
gone forever, take a breath, be sad for a
moment, and then clean the trap. You might
as well make something positive out of all
this.

7 **CLEAN THE TRAP WITH A WIRE THAT
BENDS AROUND THE CURVE.**
A coat hanger works; straighten it first!

8 IF THIS ENTIRE EXPEDITION WAS TO CLEAR A CLOG AND YOU DIDN'T FIND IT IN THE TRAP, PUSH AND TURN A DRAIN AUGER, sometimes called a plumbing snake because it looks like a long metal snake, AS FAR AS IT WILL REACH INTO THE DRAINPIPE, often called the waste pipe. Why do so many things have 2 names? It certainly makes instructions interesting—which more often than not means difficult.

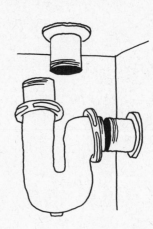

10 MAKE SURE THE WASHERS AND COUPLING NUTS ARE IN PLACE AND SCREW THE NUTS ONTO THE TRAP. Without the washers, your surprise for the day will be a big leak.

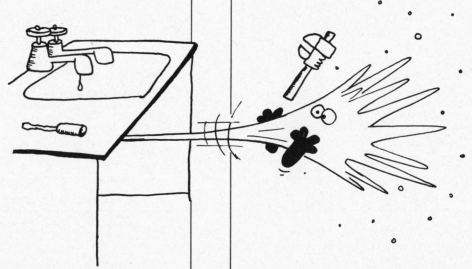

9 AFTER YOU HAVE EITHER FOUND WHAT WAS LOST OR CLEANED THE TRAP, or both, REPLACE THE TRAP BY POSITIONING IT BETWEEN THE DRAINPIPE AND THE TAILPIECE.

11 GIVE THE NUTS A TURN WITH THE WRENCH TO TIGHTEN THEM, BEING CAREFUL NOT TO OVERTIGHTEN THEM, if you can figure out what that is.

12 RUN THE WATER DOWN THE DRAIN. Pray for no leaks, no clogs, and that what you thought might have gone down the drain is really on the window sill.

It usually doesn't break, it just malfunctions—same thing as far as I'm concerned. Half the battle is not being afraid of the parts and their names.

THE POP-UP MECHANISM COMES IN 3 SECTIONS.

Read this. It will help, believe me. Better yet, memorize it.

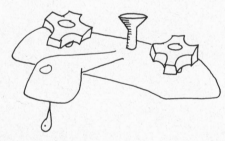

THE LIFT ROD.

At the top of this vertical rod is the control knob, which sits between the hot and cold faucets. The rod extends down under the sink. The top is the *lift*, and the bottom is the *rod*, hence lift rod. Clever!

THE CLEVIS.

Who picked this name? This is a vertical flat rod with holes in it.

THE PIVOT ROD.

This is a horizontal rod that pivots on a plastic ball inside the drain. The rod part pokes through the clevis.

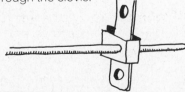

1 **WISH THERE WERE MORE ROOM UNDER THE SINK.**
Get ready to skin your knuckles and bing your head.

2 **IF THE PLUG DOES NOT MAKE A GOOD SEAL, FREE THE LIFT ROD BY LOOSENING THE SCREW AT THE TOP OF THE CLEVIS.**
Don't remove the screw; just loosen it.

3 **PRESS THE PLUG DOWN TO SEAL THE DRAIN.**
The clevis will rise—it's supposed to.

4 **PULL UP THE CONTROL KNOB AS FAR AS YOU CAN AND THEN LOWER IT 1/4″ AND RETIGHTEN THE CLEVIS SCREW.**

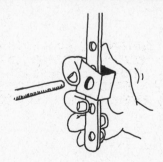

77

A

5 IF THE MECHANISM IS STICKY AND DIFFICULT TO OPERATE (how do you know this is a foregone conclusion?) SQUEEZE THE SPRING CLIP THAT HOLDS THE PIVOT ROD TO THE CLEVIS ROD WITH YOUR FINGERS.
There is only 1 spring clip down there—you can't miss it unless it's missing.

6 BACK THE PIVOT ROD OUT OF THE CLEVIS HOLE,
if you can remember which is which.

7 RESET THE PIVOT ROD IN THE NEXT HIGHER CLEVIS HOLE BY SQUEEZING THE SPRING CLIP TOGETHER AND SLIDING THE PIVOT ROD THROUGH THE CLIP ON BOTH SIDES OF THE CLEVIS.
If you forget the clip, the pivot rod will fall out with 1 push-pull of the control knob.

8 TRY THE MECHANISM. IF IT DOESN'T MAKE A TIGHT SEAL (here come my favorite instructions), REPEAT STEPS 2, 3, AND 4.
It will work. Or if all else fails, talk to it. (Whatever happened to good old-fashioned plugs?)

REMOVING A POP-UP PLUG TO CLEAN A DRAIN

After a while all the gunk that manages to go down the drain gets stuck there in a glob. Too bad the drain doesn't work like a toaster and pop up the glob.

THERE ARE 4 TYPES OF PLUGS. TYPE A AND B ARE EASY TO REMOVE;

B

THEY JUST SIT ON THE PIVOT ROD AND PULL OUT.
Unfortunately, because they aren't attached to anything, they tend to end up in other rooms of the house. At least, in my house they've ended up in closets, toy boxes, the sandbox—they're seldom in the drain. The only thing that keeps water in my sink is the clog. TYPES C AND D ARE ATTACHED TO THE PIVOT ROD, so if you can't pull out the plug, you might have...

TO REMOVE TYPE C, DISENGAGE THE PIVOT ROD FROM THE SLOT BY LIFTING THE PLUG AND TURNING IT A QUARTER-TURN CLOCKWISE.
If after a couple of tries the plug won't let go, you have the kind you'll wish you didn't have.

TO REMOVE TYPE D, FREE THE PIVOT ROD AND PULL IT OUT OF THE DRAIN TO LIBERATE THE PLUG.

1 WITH TAPE-WRAPPED PLIERS—not the whole thing, just the jaws—OR A WRENCH, UNSCREW THE RETAINING NUT THAT HOLDS THE PIVOT ROD ASSEMBLY IN THE DRAIN T.

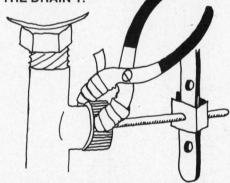

Actually, the drain T looks nothing like a "T" unless you're lying on your side.

2 SQUEEZE THE SPRING CLIP ON THE CLEVIS AND BACK THE PIVOT ROD OUT OF THE DRAIN.
At this point you probably haven't a clue what a clevis is. Look in the previous section for clues. AS YOU DO THIS, THE PLUG WILL BE RELEASED. Do it slowly; you may not have to back it all the way out and run the risk of losing the gasket and washer that make the seal. However, if they do fall out, just remember which one hit the floor first.

What to do when jiggling the handle doesn't work.

1 **REMOVE THE LID FROM THE BACK OF THE TOILET TANK.**
Don't panic when you see what's in there. It's really all quite harmless.

2 **UNSCREW THE FLOAT BALL.**
It's the only large ball in the toilet tank, unless the kids have dropped a baseball in there. **SHAKE IT TO MAKE SURE THERE'S NO WATER IN IT AND REPLACE IT.** If there's water in it, throw it away—after you've purchased a new one. **IF THE WATER IS STILL RUNNING, KEEP READING.**

3 **LIFT UP THE FLOAT BALL.**
If the water stops running, the float ball isn't floating high enough in the tank to close the float valve entirely. If the water level in the tank is too high, the extra water will be running into the overflow tube. When you lower the ball, you'll see the water heading over the top of an open tube before your very eyes.

4 **IF THE FLOAT ARM IS METAL, FIRST LOOK FOR AN ADJUSTMENT SCREW ON THE TOP OF THE WATER-INLET ASSEMBLY.**
Of course, you might see 2 screws. I always find 2 when I'm looking for 1. One is for adjusting the float, and the other one holds the float arm to the assembly. If you can't figure out which is which, the worst that can happen is that you think you're adjusting when in fact you're removing. The float ball, arm and all, will splash into the tank. Put it back and **TURN THE ADJUSTMENT SCREW TO LOWER THE FLOAT BALL. IF THERE IS NO ADJUSTMENT SCREW, BEND THE ARM DOWNWARD, SLOWLY.**
You don't want to break it or anything else it's attached to. This is simple adjusting, not heavy-duty replacing—yet.

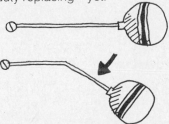

5 **IF THE FLOAT ARM IS PLASTIC, ADJUST THE LARGE PLASTIC NUT ON THE SIDE OF THE FLOAT ARM TO LOWER THE ARM AND BALL SO THAT THEY FLOAT HIGHER AND SHUT OFF THE WATER SOONER.**
Cross your fingers and hope that the running stops. If not…

6 **CHECK THE TANK BALL OR FLAPPER BALL,**
located down, way down, in the bottom of the tank. If it's worn or rough around the edges, it will not seal properly and will have to be replaced (see the section, "Replacing a Tank Ball or Flapper Ball"). If the ball appears to be in good condition, keep reading.

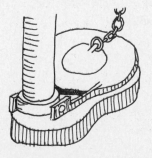

7 **IF THESE ADJUSTMENTS AND CHECKS HAVEN'T STOPPED THE RUNNING WATER, YOU MAY HAVE TO REPLACE THE WATER-INLET ASSEMBLY.**
The bad news is that something is probably wrong with the washers or valve seat. The good news is that these are inside parts, and you don't have to try to find them. You just replace the whole shebang.

REPLACING A WATER-INLET ASSEMBLY

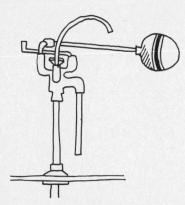

It's the mass of equipment on the left-hand side of the tank—and a lot less confusing than it looks.

1 **PURCHASE A REPLACEMENT ASSEMBLY THAT LOOKS LIKE THE ONE YOU ARE REMOVING.**
If the replacement looks complicated, get instructions from the person at the store, or ask them to show you how to replace it.

2 **SHUT OFF THE WATER-SUPPLY VALVE UNDER THE TOILET TANK.**
It's easy to find. There's only one.

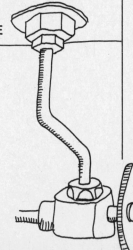

3 **FLUSH THE TOILET.**
With the water off, the tank will not refill. If it does, try to find out what you've just shut off.

4 **DRY THE TANK.**
You don't want to have to mop the floor too.

5 **REMOVE THE FLOAT BALL ARM FROM THE INLET-VALVE ASSEMBLY.**
Not only does it move up and down, it comes off.

6 **UNCLIP THE REFILL TUBE FROM THE OVERFLOW TUBE.**
The refill tube is a skinny tube that runs from the inlet-valve assembly to the overflow tube. Remember, you saw the water disappearing over its edge.

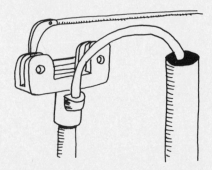

7 **ON THE UNDERSIDE OF THE TANK, UNSCREW THE COUPLING NUT AND DISCONNECT THE WATER-SUPPLY TUBE.**
Remember where you shut the water off? That's it. **LEAVE THE NUT HANGING ON THE SUPPLY TUBE.** Chances are good

that you can use it on the new assembly. Trying to get the nut off the supply tube could mean replacing the supply tube altogether. Why ask for trouble?

8 **STILL UNDER THE TANK, REMOVE THE LOCKNUT AND WASHER FROM THE THREADED END OF THE INLET-VALVE ASSEMBLY.**
Let's see, is that clockwise or counterclockwise?

9 **DON'T GIVE UP NOW, YOU'RE ALMOST THERE.**

10 **REACH INTO THE TOILET AND REMOVE THE ASSEMBLY.**
And mop up the water you left in the tank if you couldn't be bothered with Step 4.

11 **REMOVE THE NUT AND WASHER FROM THE NEW ASSEMBLY AND PLACE THE UNIT INTO THE TANK. LOOSELY REPLACE THE WASHER AND COUPLING NUT.**
The tightening part comes later. If you can reuse the nut that's hanging on the supply tube, hooray! You've saved yourself extra steps and given yourself a leftover for your junk drawer collection.

12 **CLIP THE REFILL TUBE ONTO THE TOP OF THE OVERFLOW TUBE.**
By now you know what that is.

13 **ATTACH THE FLOAT BALL ARM.**
You know what this is too. It should make you feel good when you start to recognize all the bits and pieces.

14 **NOW TIGHTEN THE LOCKNUT ON THE UNDERSIDE OF THE TANK.**
Be careful not to overtighten it. You don't want your surprise for the day to be a cracked toilet tank.

15 **ADJUST THE FLOAT ARM TO SET THE WATER LEVEL.**
See Steps 3 and 4.

16 **PAT YOURSELF ON THE BACK.**
You no longer have a running toilet. You also just saved yourself an expensive service call and got acquainted with the insides of your toilet.

17 **NOW YOU CAN REPLACE THE TANK LID AND SMILE.**
Rush out and tell someone!

Note: If you have only 1 bathroom in the house, work quickly.

REPLACING A TANK BALL OR FLAPPER BALL

WHAT are you looking for and WHERE are you looking for it? You know WHY: your toilet is running, and you've almost jiggled the handle off trying to get it to stop. It's time to get to know your toilet better.

1 REMOVE THE TANK LID, FLUSH THE TOILET, AND WATCH WHAT HAPPENS. DO THIS TWICE.
If you still don't get it, do it again. It's not scary, and it will give you a good idea how this mystery mechanism works.

2 STICK YOUR HAND INTO THE WATER. GO ON, DO IT!
Surprise! A little on the cold side, but it's clean, as clean as the water in the rest of the house. You have now overcome your water phobia, and your courage is better organized.

3 FOLLOW ALL THE STEPS IN THE SECTION, "REPAIRING A RUNNING TOILET," except do not shut off the water-supply valve **UNTIL YOU GET TO STEP 6 AND READ "SEE THE SECTION ON REPLACING A FLAPPER BALL."**
You're doing it!

4 LOOK DOWN OVER THE CENTER OF THE TANK. YOU SHOULD SEE A DARK, RUBBERY-LOOKING ROUND THING.
It's either an old tank ball or a dead-tired flapper ball—they both look like giant stop-

pers. **IF YOU SEE A SPACE-AGE PLASTIC PIECE, IT'S A TILT VALVE. PULL THE STOPPER OFF ITS BOTTOM AND TAKE IT TO THE STORE TO BUY A REPLACEMENT.**

5 FLUSH THE TOILET AGAIN AND WATCH IT WORK.
If it's a tank ball you're looking at, it should drop, freely, straight back into the outlet valve as the water descends in the tank. If it's a flapper ball, it "flaps" from its semirigid frame and should close snugly over the outlet valve.

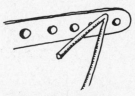

2 REMOVE THE OLD LIFT WIRES FROM THE TRIP LEVER.
There are 2 in a row, and you're going to replace them with 1 in a row.

6 CHECK THE CONDITION OF WHICH- EVER BALL YOU HAVE.
If it's a tank ball and the edges are worn or a flapper ball that isn't sealing—or flapping—properly, either one should be replaced by a flapper (not the 1920 variety—I just had to put that somewhere in here).

7 PURCHASE A NEW FLAPPER BALL.
If you wonder about the size of the replacement, you could take the old ball to the store—or take the toilet.

8 SHUT OFF THE WATER-SUPPLY VALVE ON THE UNDERSIDE OF THE TANK.

9 FLUSH THE TOILET TO DRAIN IT.
You can watch it again if you still didn't get it the first, second, or third time. At this point the rest of the family will be wondering what's up in the bathroom.

3 LOCATE THE OVERFLOW TUBE.
It's an open-ended vertical tube that stands next to the tank ball, or where the tank ball just was. **LOOK AT THE BASE OF THE TUBE FOR WHAT LOOKS LIKE A COLLAR:** it's called a guidepost—who would have guessed? **LOOSEN THE THUMB-SCREW** (can anyone unscrew anything with just their thumb?) **THAT FASTENS THE GUIDEPOST TO THE OVERFLOW TUBE.**

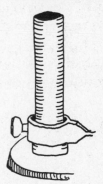

REPLACING AN OLD TANK BALL WITH A FLAPPER BALL

It's a good idea because a flapper ball is less prone to misalignment and being knocked out of position by all the water rushing around in the tank.

1 UNSCREW THE TANK BALL FROM ITS LIFT WIRE.

4 REMOVE THE GUIDEPOST AND ARM FROM THE TUBE. YOU'LL RUN THE GUIDEPOST UP THE TUBE TO MEET THE SKINNY LITTLE REFILL TUBE.
Don't panic, **JUST UNCLIP THE REFILL TUBE, REMOVE THE GUIDEPOST, AND CLIP THE TUBE BACK ONTO THE OVER-FLOW TUBE.**
That kind of thing used to stop me cold. I was convinced that if it wasn't in the instructions, it was something I wasn't supposed to do. I was overwhelmed by a sense of wrecking things.

5 SLIP THE COLLAR OF THE NEW FLAP-PER BALL TO THE BOTTOM OF THE OVERFLOW TUBE.
You'll have to unclip and clip the refill tube again; just consider it something you're good at now.

6 **TIGHTEN THE THUMBSCREW ON THE COLLAR—**
with two thumbs.

7 **HOOK THE CHAIN FROM THE BALL THROUGH A HOLE IN THE TRIP LEVER DIRECTLY OVER THE FLAPPER, LEAVING ABOUT 1/2″ OF SLACK.**
How you measure this is beyond me!

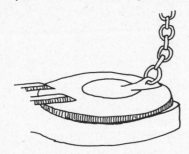

8 **TURN ON THE WATER-SUPPLY VALVE.**

9 **FLUSH THE TOILET AND WATCH TO SEE IF THE TANK DRAINS COMPLETELY—ALMOST.**
If it doesn't, take up a little slack in the chain or reposition the chain in another trip lever hole. You may have to fiddle with these 2 adjustments, but don't give up. Somewhere between the chain and the holes is a solution. After all this, your days of handle jiggling will be over.

REPLACING AN OLD FLAPPER BALL WITH A NEW ONE

Hope this is what you're doing, because it's easy.

1 **ONCE THE TANK IS DRAINED, UNHOOK THE OLD FLAPPER BALL FROM THE COLLAR AND UNHOOK THE CHAIN ATTACHED TO THE TRIP LEVER.**

2 **TAKE THE FLAPPER BALL TO THE STORE IF YOU'RE WORRIED ABOUT THE REPLACEMENT.**

3 **HOOK THE NEW FLAPPER BALL TO THE COLLAR, REPOSITION THE CHAIN, TURN ON THE WATER, PRACTICE FLUSHING, AND CHEER.**
Told you that was easy!

If the plumbing law of averages holds true, this will break only on a Sunday, a holiday, or in the middle of the night.

1 **SHUT OFF THE WATER-SUPPLY VALVE UNDER THE TOILET.**
You can change the handle without getting rid of all the water in the tank, but if you're still squeamish about fishing around in there, don't do it. Other than changing the seat, there's very little you can do to a toilet with the tank full, except clean it or change the toilet paper roll. (Have you ever noticed that you're the only one in the house who knows how to install a new roll of toilet paper?)

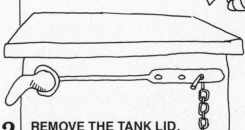

2 **REMOVE THE TANK LID.**
The rest of the flush handle lives in the tank. Inside the tank the flush handle turns into the trip lever, a horizontal rod with either holes or a groove in the end farthest away from the handle. You can't miss it—the only other horizontal rod in the tank is the one with the large ball on the end of it.

3 FLUSH THE TOILET TO DRAIN IT.
If there isn't 1 more flush left in the handle, pull up on the chain or lift rod attached to the trip lever to open the valve at the bottom of the tank. Or get a pot and bail, or try to figure out how to siphon.

4 REMOVE THE CHAIN OR LIFT ROD FROM THE END OF THE TRIP LEVER.

5 TAKE A GOOD LOOK AT WHAT'S LEFT.
It is probably as simple as a plastic or metal trip lever attached to the handle tailpiece—the threaded part of the handle just inside the tank—all held in place by a locknut snugged up to the inside of the tank wall.

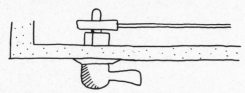

6 UNSCREW THE LOCKNUT NEXT TO THE INSIDE OF THE TANK WALL ON THE TAILPIECE.
If there's a washer, don't lose it. If there isn't a washer, the manufacturer probably forgot it. REMOVE THE HANDLE BY PULLING IT OUT OF ITS HOLE FROM THE FRONT OF THE TANK. This is the only way it comes out—no decisions, no choices, just out!

7 TAKE THE OLD HANDLE TO THE STORE AND BUY A REPLACEMENT.
Or if you're a good guesser, you could have bought the replacement earlier. I hate guessing trips because they almost always amount to more than one.

8 INSERT THE NEW HANDLE.
If there was a flange—what a great word for a flat, round support piece—between the handle and the outside of the tank, put it back, **AND PUT EVERYTHING BACK TOGETHER IN THE SAME ORDER THAT IT CAME OFF. WHEN YOU GET TO REPLACING THE LOCKNUT AND TIGHTENING IT, REMEMBER: TOO TIGHT AND YOU'LL CRACK THE TANK,** or break the handle.

9 REPLACE THE TANK LID, FLUSH THE TOILET, AND REMEMBER THAT YOU FORGOT TO TURN THE WATER ON.

Things you learned and might like to remember for next time.

FAUCETS

*When what turns off
the water, doesn't!*

CHANGING A FAUCET WASHER

Almost always the cause of that "drive you crazy" drip when a faucet in the off position isn't. Or how I broke my sink the first time because it didn't look like the book.

HELPFUL HINT
ON A STRIP OF MASKING TAPE, LINE UP THE PARTS AS YOU RE- MOVE THEM TO HELP YOU REMEM- BER THE ORDER THEY GO BACK ON WHEN YOU'VE FINISHED YOUR REPAIR. Sometimes a hint is more helpful at the beginning; in this case a hint at the end may be a hint too late.

1 **ORGANIZE EVERY SPONGE, BUCKET, AND MOP YOU HAVE IN THE HOUSE.**
Plumbing is more often than not synonymous with water everywhere.

2 **DETERMINE WHICH TAP IS DRIPPING BY FEELING THE DRIPS.**
Do this now before you turn off the water. Who needs to change the washers on both faucets? If it's the hot water tap, just think of all the money you're sending down the drain. It will give you the incentive to keep going.

3 **TURN OFF THE WATER TO THE SINK YOU'RE WORKING ON.**
If today is your lucky day, the shut-off valve will be right under the sink. If not, you'll have to turn off the main water supply to the house. That's somewhere in the basement; hunt around and find the place where the water enters the house from the street. It's a pipe with a valve on it—it's there, I promise!

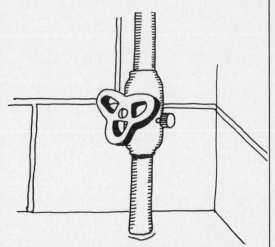

4 **IF YOU HAD TO TURN OFF THE MAIN WATER SUPPLY, DRAIN THE SYSTEM BY TURNING ON A FAUCET ON EACH LEVEL OF THE HOUSE. IN ANY EVENT, OPEN THE TAPS ON THE SINK YOU'RE WORKING ON AND LEAVE THEM OPEN.**
What you are avoiding is a puddle or geyser and having to use your sponges and mops.

5 **WHEN NO MORE WATER IS COMING OUT OF THE FAUCET, CLOSE THE SINK DRAIN,**
just in case you remove something and it gets away from you. Your surprise for the day will be removing the trap to retrieve it (see the section on removing traps).

6 **COUNT TO 3, TAKE A BIG BREATH, AND . . .**

7 **REMOVE THE SMALL PLASTIC DECO- RATIVE CAP FROM THE CENTER OF THE HANDLE.**
You'll recognize it—it has an "H" or "C" or some reasonable facsimile stamped on it. A pointed nail file is a good tool for this job.

8 REMOVE THE SCREW YOU'RE LOOKING AT IN THE CENTER OF THE HANDLE.
It holds the handle in place.

9 REMOVE THE HANDLE BY PULLING STRAIGHT UP.
So far, so good.

10 IF WHAT YOU'RE LOOKING AT IS SIMPLE AND DECORATIVE, IT'S THE *DECORATIVE BONNET*. REMOVE IT.

11 IF WHAT YOU'RE LOOKING AT IS COMPLICATED, DON'T PANIC.
You're on the right track. This is the top part of the spindle or stem assembly.

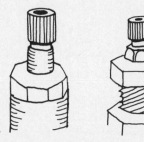

12 LOOSEN THE PACKING NUT BY TURNING IT COUNTERCLOCKWISE WITH A WRENCH.
This sounds simple, and it is if you're looking at only 1 nut. However, if you've uncovered a small nut at the top and a large nut under it, it's the large nut you want. The small nut is the stem nut; leave it alone. To make matters worse, you might find a decorative thing sitting on the sink surface that looks like it could be a nut of some kind. (It isn't. I know—I broke my sink trying to remove it.) That, in fact, is the housing for the entire stem assembly. All you're after is the large nut that is somewhat centrally located on the piece that's poking out of the sink.

13 UNSCREW THE STEM OR SPINDLE (why does everything have 2 names? Pick the one you like) **BY HAND AND LOOK AT ITS BOTTOM.**
Eureka! You have finally found the washer.

14 IF YOU HAVE LOTS OF NEW WASHERS HANGING AROUND (fat chance), **FIND ONE THAT FITS, BUT IF YOU HAVE ANY DOUBTS ABOUT THE SIZE OF THE REPLACEMENT WASHER, TAKE THE ENTIRE ASSEMBLY TO THE STORE AND BUY ONE THAT FITS.**
Unfortunately, new washers don't come in "ones"; they come in packages of lots. Smile at the person in the store—maybe you can buy just one. Smile again, and they might put the new washer on for you. If not...

15 REMOVE THE BRASS SCREW AT THE BASE OF THE ASSEMBLY AND REPLACE THE OLD WASHER.
You've done it—almost!

16 REPLACE THE BRASS SCREW AND GO THROUGH ALL THESE STEPS IN REVERSE ORDER TO GET THE FAUCET OPERATIONAL.
This is where the **HELPFUL HINT** can really be helpful, especially if your memory is anything like mine.

17 TURN ON THE WATER SUPPLY. CROSS YOUR FINGERS AND HOPE THE DRIP DIED.

18 OOPS! RUSH AROUND THE HOUSE TURNING OFF ALL THE OPEN FAUCETS.
Hope like mad that you left the plugs out of those drains. If you didn't, you've just forgotten your accomplishment and are now the mop brigade!

CHANGING A WASHER IN A CARTRIDGE-STEM FAUCET

You know you have one if you get all the way to Step 13 under ''Changing a Faucet Washer'' and discover that the stem doesn't unscrew—it pulls out.

1 AS YOU LIFT THE CARTRIDGE OUT OF THE FAUCET BODY—that's the piece still left in the sink—NOTICE THE 2 KEYS ON THE SIDE OF THE STEM.

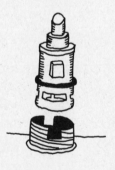

They're permanent, to keep them from getting lost. **NOTICE ALSO THE 2 COR-RESPONDING** *KEYWAY* **SLOTS ON THE FAUCET BODY.** This gives you some idea how to get it to go back in there.

2 LOOK INTO THE FAUCET BODY. You'll see the washer. WITH A PAIR OF NEEDLE-NOSE PLIERS, PULL OUT THE RUBBER WASHER AND THE SPRING THAT LIVES UNDER IT.

3 REPLACE THE SPRING WITH A NEW ONE. Old parts tend to break the next week or the next day or as soon as you put the whole assembly back together again.

4 PUSH THE NEW WASHER FIRMLY INTO PLACE WITH YOUR INDEX FINGER, or whatever finger you wish. (You could use your thumb if it fits in the hole.)

5 REPLACE THE CARTRIDGE. If the faucet still drips, you may have to replace the cartridge. Just take it to the store and ask, ''Do you have one of these?'' Unfortunately and invariably, it's the only one that's out of stock, and you'll have to put up with the drip for another 6 weeks.

ELIMINATING DRIPS, LEAKS, AND ANY EXTRANEOUS WATER FROM A SINGLE-LEVER FAUCET

This is the faucet you love to use when your hands are either filthy or full and all you have left to turn on the water with is a good, swift elbow.

If the drips are coming from the faucet that's supposed to be off and isn't, quite, CHANGE THE VALVE SEATS.

If the drip looks more like a leak and dribbles from the base of the faucet assembly, see the section, "Replacing O-Rings in a Single-Lever Faucet."

1 FIND (this could make Step 1 a 20-minute project) **A PENCIL, PEN, MARKER, OR COLOR CRAYON AND A PIECE OF PAPER.**
You are going to make a diagram of what you are about to dismantle, or if you don't get it back together, your last will and testament.

2 **TURN OFF THE WATER SUPPLY TO THE SINK.**
You hope the valve is under the sink. If not, it's off to the basement to find (there's that word again—maybe 10 minutes this time) the main water-supply valve. Hunt around; it's down there somewhere. They should be painted red with a sign over them!

3 **DRAIN THE SYSTEM BY TURNING ON A FAUCET ON EACH LEVEL OF THE HOUSE. CHECK TO SEE THAT THE DRAINS IN THOSE SINKS ARE OPEN. IMPORTANT NOW—YOU'LL SEE WHY LATER,**
or maybe you've guessed it!

4 **OPEN AND DRAIN THE FAUCET YOU ARE GOING TO WORK ON, AND ONCE ALL THE WATER STOPS RUNNING, PLUG THE SINK DRAIN IMMEDIATELY.**
Forget to do this, and you may never get a good look at what you were trying to replace.

REPLACING VALVE SEATS IN A ROTATING-BALL ASSEMBLY IN A SINGLE-LEVER FAUCET

This probably means absolutely nothing to you, but more often than not this is the faucet you have in the kitchen where *your* hands are full and *everyone else's* are filthy. Teach everyone in the family the elbow trick!

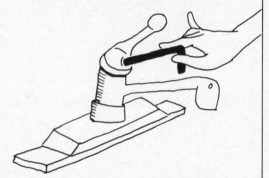

5 **FIND,** how about **LOCATE, WHAT LOOKS LIKE A SMALL HOLE ON THE UNDERSIDE OF THE LEVER.**
It may be hidden by a layer of grot—clean it. You are now officially doing 2 jobs at once. This is what most books forget: it's never just fixing. It's fixing and cleaning, or cleaning and fixing.

6 **NOW THAT THE FAUCET IS CLEAN, YOU'LL SEE THE BRAND NAME STAMPED ON THE UNIT. REMEMBER IT. STOP!**
Before you rush to the store to buy the replacement parts, read Steps 8 and 9 first. They'll save you a trip.

7 **LOOK INTO THE HOLE.**
Yuck! Clean it out—you need to get in there.

8 **IF YOU WERE EXPECTING TO SEE AN ORDINARY SCREW,** forget it. **WHAT YOU ARE LOOKING AT IN THAT SHINY CLEAN HOLE IS A HEX SCREW THAT MUST BE LOOSENED WITH A HEX WRENCH—**
not a pointed knife or fork tine. Improvise

and you'll kill the screw head; it will never come off, certainly not in this life.

9 **NOW GO TO THE STORE** (see—one trip) **AND BUY A HEX WRENCH.**
Ask at the store which one; they come in every size imaginable, not "1 size fits all." Also buy **REPLACEMENT PARTS SPECIFIC TO THE FAUCET YOU HAVE.** You may not have seen or cared about the brand name for years. You do now.

10 **LOOSEN THE SCREW WITH THE HEX WRENCH, BUT *DON'T REMOVE IT.***
You'll lose it. You don't want to replace the hex screw, just the valve seats.

11 **GET YOUR PENCIL AND PAPER READY. FROM HERE ON IN, REMEMBER HOW THINGS COME OUT AND DRAW WHAT YOU SEE BEFORE YOU REMOVE ANYTHING.**
You don't need to be Michelangelo; you're only drawing what *you* need to recognize.

12 **WITH TAPE-WRAPPED PLIERS** (just the jaws), **UNSCREW THE CAP AND LIFT OUT THE STEM OF THE BALL. WATCH IT—IT COMES WITH THE CAM ASSEMBLY.**
It's part plastic and part rubber, and it sits on top of the ball. Draw away, Picasso!

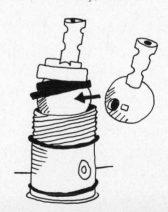

13 | LOOK INTO WHAT'S LEFT IN THE FAUCET.

The 2 rubber eyes staring back at you are the valve seats.

14 | WITH NEEDLE-NOSE PLIERS, REMOVE THE VALVE SEATS AND THE SPRINGS UNDER THEM.

It's all right to lose these—you've got new ones.

15 | PUSH NEW SPRINGS (you don't want to worry about anything old under the new valve seats; you'll wake up every morning and wonder how the springs are holding up) AND NEW VALVE SEATS INTO PLACE WITH YOUR FINGERS.

Easier said than done. Small springs and small valve seats tend to go everywhere but into small holes. Patience!

16 | TAKE A GOOD LOOK AT THE BALL. IF IT IS CORRODED OR ROUGH, GET A NEW ONE.

No doubt it will malfunction almost before you can get the assembly back together again.

17 | REPLACE THE BALL.

There should be a tiny metal peg sticking out of the cavity. This peg fits into the oblong slot on the ball.

18 | REPLACE THE CAM ASSEMBLY.

Here is where your work of art comes in handy. On one side of the cam assembly is a small tab that fits into the corresponding slot on the faucet body. The rubber part goes in first; otherwise, you'll be trying to put this thing on upside down.

19 | SCREW ON THE CAP ASSEMBLY.

20 | BEFORE ATTACHING THE HANDLE, MOVE THE BALL'S STEM TO THE "ON" POSITION.

No leaks should spring. Of course no leaks will spring—the water's off. So turn on the water. **WAIT.** Check to make sure all the parts you replaced are tight. Now it's okay, honest. **IF YOU GET A LEAK, WITH THE TIP OF A SMALL SCREWDRIVER TIGHTEN THE ADJUSTING RING** (it's hiding in the cap) **BY TURNING IT CLOCKWISE.** If this doesn't plug the dike, you may have to replace the cam assembly. Having gone this far, you'll be happy to replace it just to see the whole thing work, minus the drips.

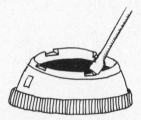

21 | POSITION THE HANDLE SO THAT THE HEX SCREW IS OVER THE FLAT AREA ON THE BALL STEM AND TIGHTEN THE HEX SCREW.

If you're looking around for the screw, it's looking at you. Remember, you left it in the handle for safekeeping.

22 | GET YOUR ELBOWS READY AND TURN ON THE FAUCET.

Hooray—no leaks! But you hear water running somewhere.

23 | RUN (fast, quick) AND TURN OFF ALL THOSE FAUCETS YOU OPENED TO DRAIN THE SYSTEM.

You'll be so glad you checked to make sure the drains were open. If you forgot, you'll have to wade to the sinks to turn off the faucets. Get out the mops!

What to do when the faucet itself isn't dripping, but the base is.

1 **COMPLETE STEPS 1 TO 10 IN THE SECTION, "ELIMINATING DRIPS, LEAKS, AND ANY EXTRANEOUS WATER FROM SINGLE-LEVER FAUCETS."**
I hate cross-referencing, but your reading it is more efficient than my rewriting it. This is not a good time for me to leave anything out; I might turn your sink into Niagara Falls, or you might have to turn it into a decorative fountain.

2 **WITH TAPE-WRAPPED PLIERS, CARE-FULLY REMOVE THE CAP AND THEN THE CAM ASSEMBLY.**
It's the part-plastic, part-rubber piece

perched on top of the rotating ball.

3 **IF YOU CAN, LEAVE THE ROTATING BALL IN PLACE. BUT IF YOU KNOW IT'S ONLY GOING TO BOUNCE OUT ANYWAY, TAKE IT OUT NOW.**
Just remember how it goes back into the faucet body, or wait until you get to Step 8 and I'll tell you what to do. Funny, I bet you chose waiting rather than remembering!

4 **TWIST AND LIFT THE SPOUT BODY UP AND OFF THE STEM TO EXPOSE THE O-RINGS.**
Hooray! You'll be filled with that wonderful feeling of success that comes from working like mad, hoping to find what you've never even seen, and then there they are—2 rubber rings on the piece still stuck in the sink.

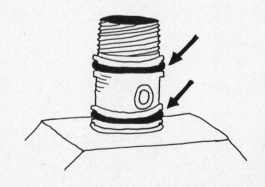

5 REMOVE THE OLD O-RINGS. IF YOU DON'T HAVE NEW ONES, TAKE THE OLD ONES TO THE STORE AND ASK FOR EXACT REPLACEMENTS. DON'T THROW THEM AWAY,
even if you know the brand name. The store may be temporarily out of stock, and you'll not only have no O-rings, you'll have no faucet, and "temporarily" can mean "a long time." Just think about washing dishes in your bathroom sink. **BUY 5.** Five small rubber rings may start out 5 in the store, but arrive home—4; get to the sink—3. That's just the number you need: 1 for wrecking and 2 to make it into place. Of course, they may come in packages of 10, in which case you can afford to drop them all the way home and still wreck a couple.

6 PUT PETROLEUM JELLY ON THE BODY OF THE FAUCET BEFORE INSTALLING THE NEW O-RINGS TO PREVENT THEM FROM TEARING.
You don't have to worry. You're prepared, you have extras!

7 REPLACE THE SPOUT BODY BY PUSHING DOWN GENTLY AND TWISTING AT THE SAME TIME.
With the petroleum jelly gooped on the body, it should go on more easily than it came off. Check to make sure the faucet isn't aiming at your face. It's easier to put it on "upside right" (right side up) now than it will be once you have all the pieces back together.

8 TO REPLACE THE BALL, CAM ASSEMBLY, CAP, AND HANDLE, SEE STEPS 8 TO 21 IN THE SECTION ON REPLACING VALVE SEATS IN A ROTATING BALL.
Told you I'd tell you.

9 TO DEAL WITH ANY EXTRANEOUS WATER, SEE STEP 23 IN THE SAME SECTION.
Be prepared—read with the mop in your hand.

The "what else" in the bathroom that could possibly spring a drip.

You know you have one when you step into the shower one morning, know you haven't turned it on yet, and something drips on you. Hope it's not from a crack in the ceiling. Somehow, thinking the worst first floods you with a tremendous sense of relief when you discover it's not.

1 LOCATE THE SOURCE OF THE DRIP, THEN FIDDLE WITH THE SHOWER HEAD TO SEE HOW IT'S ATTACHED TO THE SHOWER ARM (the bent piece of pipe that comes at you out of the wall). **IF THE LEAK IS ABOVE THE SWIVEL** (what a wonderful word, swivel), **STEPS 2 AND 3 ARE YOURS. IF THE LEAK IS BETWEEN THE SWIVEL AND THE SHOWER HEAD, YOU GET STEPS 4 AND 5.**
Everyone gets 2, so no one will feel left out.

2 IF THE LEAK IS NORTH OF THE SHOWER HEAD WHERE THE SWIVEL IS ATTACHED TO THE SHOWER ARM, TAPE THE NUT AT THE TOP OF THE

SWIVEL WITH MASKING TAPE TO PREVENT SCRATCHES, AND WITH A WRENCH UNSCREW THE NUT COUNTERCLOCKWISE.
Good luck—if you don't know which way is which, you could put the shower head on forever. The leak is then the least of your problems. **REMOVE THE SHOWER HEAD.**

3 APPLY PIPE SEALANT OR TEFLON PIPE TAPE TO THE THREADS OF THE SHOWER ARM TO MAKE A GOOD DRIP-PROOF SEAL.
I love Teflon tape. You don't have to be neat or spend forever looking for your scissors—just wrap it around the threads a couple of times in the direction of the threads, and a good yank will tear it off. **DON'T LET GO OF THE ROLL.**

4 REPLACE THE SHOWER HEAD.
Hand-tight is good enough. Too tight and it's there forever—maybe 1 turn of the wrench, just in case.

5 **IF THE LEAK IS COMING FROM THE SPACE BETWEEN THE SWIVEL AND THE HEAD ITSELF, YOU HAVE EITHER A WASHER OR AN O-RING TO REPLACE.** (O-ring is a wonderful word—it's descriptive, but a little redundant.)

6 **TO REMOVE THE SHOWER HEAD, TAPE THE LOCKING COLLAR** (either a ridged collar or a large nut) **WITH MASKING TAPE. WITH A WRENCH FOR THE NUT OR PLIERS FOR THE RIDGED COLLAR, UNSCREW IT COUNTERCLOCKWISE.** You have to hold onto the shower head while you do this, and bear in mind that shower heads do not like to come apart easily.

7 **LOCATE THE WASHER OR O-RING INSIDE THE COLLAR OR NUT AND REPLACE IT WITH A NEW ONE.**

8 **REASSEMBLE THE SHOWER HEAD USING PIPE SEALANT OR TEFLON TAPE ON THE THREADS, STAND BACK, AND WAIT FOR THE DRIP YOU HOPE WILL NEVER COME.**

HELPFUL HINT
TO CLEAN A SHOWER HEAD, REMOVE THE HEAD FROM THE SHOWER ARM AND SOAK IT IN VINEGAR TO REMOVE ALL THE MINERAL DEPOSITS THAT EVENTUALLY PLUG IT UP.

Things you learned and might like to remember for next time.

CLOGS

The things that render plugs unnecessary!

REMOVING A CLOG FROM A SINK OR TUB

In every case you know you have one when the yucky water hangs around instead of disappearing down the drain.

1 **FIRST FIND YOUR HANDY-DANDY PLUNGER,** also called a plumber's helper or plumber's friend. In this case it's *your* friend because you need help and guess who's the plumber!

2 **REMOVE THE STOPPER OR METAL PLUG,** if there is one, **FROM THE DRAIN.** It's not keeping the water from going down the drain anyway, the clog is.

3 **COVER THE DRAIN WITH 1″ or 2″ OF WATER.** Of course, you might already have 5″ or 6″ of water looking back at you. If so, ignore this step and read on.

4 **COVER THE OVERFLOW HOLE WITH A WET CLOTH.** This hole is usually located under the faucet—it's what keeps you from having a lovely deep tubbie and keeps the kids from flooding the sink.

5 **COVER THE RIM ON THE BOTTOM OF THE PLUNGER'S RUBBER CUP WITH PETROLEUM JELLY.** This helps make a tighter seal around the drain.

6 **SUBMERGE THE RUBBER CUP OF THE PLUNGER, TIP IT ON ITS EDGE TO GET RID OF ANY AIR, AND THEN PLACE THE PLUNGER DIRECTLY OVER THE DRAIN.** By plugging the overflow and covering the cup with water, you get rid of any air that would dissipate the force necessary to clear the clog. And it does take force, believe me!

7 **PLUNGE** (hence the name plunger—maybe this makes you the plungee) **THE PLUNGER DOWN AND PULL IT UP FIRMLY SEVERAL TIMES WITHOUT PULLING THE CUP ABOVE THE WATER LEVEL** (good luck), **THEN PULL IT OFF THE DRAIN TO DRAW UP THE CLOG—** you hope. I count. A "down-up" is "1," so it goes: "1, 2, 3," and on "4" pull up on the plunger for all you're worth. I'll bet you

thought the blob goes down, not up. Does it really matter? All you care about is "gone."

8 | **DO THIS SEVERAL TIMES.**
Cross your fingers, talk to it, do anything that makes you feel that success is only 1 plunge away.

9 | **WHEN YOUR ARMS ARE TIRED AND THE WATER IS STILL SITTING THERE, DON'T GIVE UP. JUST KEEP READING.**
This has to do with "If there's a will, there *is* a way!"

10 | **YOU COULD TRY A COMMERCIAL DRAIN CLEANER.**
I personally don't like things that are covered with warning labels. They're potentially dangerous—that's why they're covered with warning labels. So **FOLLOW THE IN-STRUCTIONS.** This is no time to improvise; a little is good, and a lot could wreck your pipes.

11 | **IF THE WATER STILL REFUSES TO MOVE, USE A SINK AUGER.**
This is also called a plumber's snake. Since you're the plumber today, it's your snake.

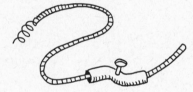

12 | **PUSH AND ROTATE THE SNAKE INTO THE DRAIN.**
This is easier said than done. If your arms are pooped from plunging, just hang around watching the water until the strength returns to your arms before you begin snake wres-tling. The snake will snake its way around the curve in the trap and cut its way through the clog. If not, your drain now has a clog and a snake stuck in it.

13 | **YOU COULD AIM YOUR GARDEN HOSE DOWN THE DRAIN. JUST BE CAREFUL AS YOU TURN UP THE PRESSURE.**
You don't want to blow the trap off. Still got water sitting there?

14 | **YOU MAY HAVE TO REMOVE THE TRAP CLEAN-OUT PLUG,** if you have one, **OR REMOVE THE TRAP AND PUSH THE AUGER BEYOND THE TRAP AND INTO THE WASTE PIPE.**
See the section on removing a trap.

15 | **IF YOU STILL HAVE WATER IN THE SINK, ADD SOIL AND TURN IT INTO A SMALL FLOWER GARDEN WHILE YOU TRY TO FIGURE OUT YOUR PLUMBING LAYOUT AND ANOTHER ROUTE TO GET AT THE CLOG.**

16 | **IF YOU HAVE MANAGED TO CLEAR THE CLOG WITHOUT HAVING DYNAMITED THE PIPES, RUN LOTS OF HOT WATER INTO THE DRAIN TO CLEAR AWAY ANY DEBRIS.**
Every month send some baking soda down the drain to keep it from getting to that "Oh no, not again" stage.

HELPFUL HINT
NEVER POUR GREASE DOWN THE DRAIN. BUT IF YOU DO, A VERY HOT, SOAPY WATER CHASER SHOULD BREAK UP THE GREASE. Then stand on guard over the sink so no one else does it!

101

UNCLOGGING A TOILET

So far I've discovered that a toy car, a tennis ball, a pair of socks, and a toothbrush make excellent clogs. To find the toothbrush I had to remove the toilet. DON'T USE A COMMERCIAL DRAIN CLEANER IN THE TOILET; it will eat the porcelain, and you'll have to replace the toilet.

1 **HOPE THAT THE WATER ISN'T FLOODING OVER THE TOILET RIM.**
If it is, don't stand there and watch it. Grab every available towel, throw them on the floor, and run to the kitchen. Grab a pot, run back to the bathroom, and bail out the toilet until it's about half full. If you try to use a plunger with the toilet full of water, you'll discover that it's one of those mistakes you only make once. Of course, you'll ask as you stand there with a pot full of water, "Now what do I do with this?" Amazing how solutions come to you when you're under duress!

2 **PLACE THE PLUNGER** (hopefully you have one with a fold-out or extra lip—they're better; at any rate, use whatever you have) **OVER THE LARGE OPENING NEAR THE BOTTOM OF THE BOWL.**
Of course, where else would you put it?

3 **WITH SHORT, RAPID STROKES, PUMP THE PLUNGER UP AND DOWN 10 TIMES.**
Actually, it's down-up; each down-up counts as 1. (If it were 10 downs and 10 ups, that would be 20 times, and you'd fall into the toilet from sheer exhaustion.) **THEN LIFT THE PLUNGER OUT OF THE WATER QUICKLY WITH A CERTAIN AMOUNT OF OOMPH.** If the water rushes down the drain, you may have cleared the obstruction. You could pour the pot of water into the toilet; if that disappears, you've done it. If not, repeat Step 3 several times—"several" depends solely on how much your back and arms ache. If the water won't budge...

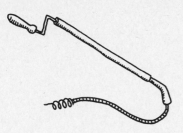

4 **USE A TOILET AUGER,**
sometimes called a *closet auger*—maybe because they're kept in closets? I wish they could remove closet clogs. I'd love to whirr one around in my daughter's closet occasionally. Actually, it's a British term. In England bathrooms are *water closets*—really toilet closets. There's no end to the information gleaned while plumbing. And that's enough of Step 4!

5 **TO USE A TOILET AUGER, WRAP YOUR HAND IN A PLASTIC GARBAGE BAG AND GUIDE THE TIP OF THE AUGER INTO THE DRAIN OPENING.**
Some toilets have the drain opening at the front of the toilet, and others have it toward the rear. **HOLD THE AUGER SLEEVE FIRMLY NEAR THE TOP AND CRANK THE AUGER HOOK SLOWLY, CLOCKWISE, INTO THE TRAP UNTIL YOU'VE EITHER HOOKED OR BROKEN THE CLOG.** You'll know you've done it when the water finally leaves the bowl.

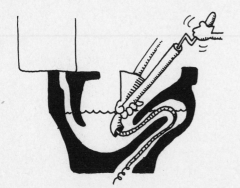

6 **CROSS YOUR FINGERS, SCOOT THE TOWELS CLOSE TO THE TOILET, GET YOUR TRUSTY POT READY, AND FLUSH THE TOILET.**
If the water disappears, cheer, pat yourself on the back, and put your auger back in the closet.

HELPFUL HINT
USE A DENTURE TABLET TO CLEAN THE TOILET.

REPAIRING A SMALL HOLE OR LEAK IN A COPPER PIPE

The only advantage to having your laundry room in the basement is that if the pipes down there are exposed, you'll probably discover a leaky pipe before your basement is transformed into a swimming pool. My laundry room is not in the basement. I never go down there unless I absolutely have to, and once when I had to go down to change a fuse, I found myself wading to the fuse box. Knowing that water and electricity don't mix, I immediately forgot about the fuse, bailed the basement, and repaired the pipe. Of course, pipes you can see are certainly easier to repair than pipes in the walls or ceilings. In this case, you have to turn off the water, make a hole in the wall or ceiling, repair the pipe, and replace the wall!

1 **TURN OFF THE MAIN WATER-SUPPLY VALVE.**
You're already in the basement, so at least it doesn't involve going too far to find the valve. Make use of any consolation, no matter how small, to pick up your spirits!

2 **DRY THE PIPE THOROUGHLY IN THE AREA AROUND THE LEAK.**
Hair dryers are terrific pipe dryers; on your hair they are marginal.

3 **IF THE LEAK IS A TINY HOLE, MAKE AN EMERGENCY PLUG BY JAMMING A PENCIL INTO THE HOLE AND BREAKING OFF THE TIP.**
The graphite point will conform to the hole and seal the leak. Of course, if your house is

anything like mine, you have to sharpen the pencil before you can do this.

4 **AS A TEMPORARY SOLUTION, APPLY EITHER EPOXY GLUE OR SOLID EPOXY PUTTY TO THE HOLE OR COVER THE HOLE WITH PLASTIC TAPE.**
If you use tape, extend it several inches on both sides of the leak. **OR SPLIT A PIECE OF RUBBER HOSE** (if you have to split a piece off your good hose, see the section on "Repairing a Garden Hose." (That's your next job.) **PUT IT AROUND THE PIPE AND SECURE IT WITH AT LEAST 3 HOSE CLAMPS.** If you don't have hose

clamps, you could use picture-hanging wire to make clamps. These repairs should suffice until Monday morning when the plumbing supply store opens. You will no doubt spend a certain part of your day checking the leak and changing the buckets.

5 **IF YOU AREN'T READY TO REPLACE THE SECTION OF PIPE** (in other words, you put things off until you're sure you know what you're doing), **BUY A PIPE SLEEVE AT THE STORE. FIT THE SLEEVE AROUND THE PIPE AND TIGHTEN THE NUTS AND BOLTS.**
The sleeve has a rubber lining that makes a seal around the hole. Be careful not to over-

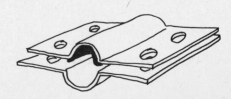

tighten the nuts and bolts; copper pipe is easily smushed. Pipe sleeves also come in various sizes, so make sure you get one that fits the diameter of your leaky pipe.

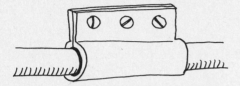

6 **IF THE LEAK HAS SPRUNG FROM A THREADED JOINT, DRY THE AREA THOROUGHLY AND APPLY EITHER EPOXY GLUE OR EPOXY PUTTY OVER THE JOINT.**
Let it dry before you turn the water on or you'll end up with a sticky leak!

HELPFUL HINTS FOR THAWING FROZEN PIPES
WRAP A HEATING PAD AROUND THE PIPE.

HEAT THE PIPE WITH A HAIR DRYER.

WRAP TOWELS AROUND THE PIPE AND POUR BOILING WATER OVER THE TOWELS. Read a good book while you wait for the pipes to thaw.

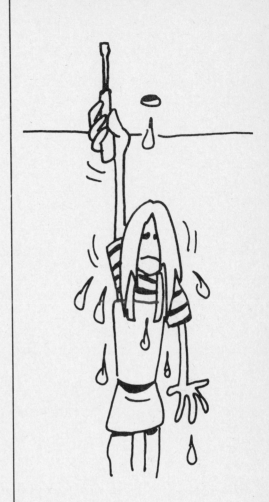

HELPFUL HINT
IF A LEAK SPRINGS OVER AN ELECTRIC CEILING FIXTURE, you'll recognize either the stain on the ceiling or the water dripping on your head. TURN OFF THE POWER IMMEDIATELY. PUT A PLASTIC DROP CLOTH ON THE FLOOR. REMOVE THE FIXTURE COVER PLATE. POKE A SMALL HOLE IN THE CEILING TO DRAIN THE WATER and get out of the way. You don't know how much water is up there. Oh, and put a bucket under it, just in case!

Things you learned and might like to remember for next time.

Extended outdoor plumbing.

REPAIRING A GARDEN HOSE

How to save and reuse what's left even if it's in 3 pieces (or 4 or 5—maybe 5's going a bit too far; buy a new hose and use the old one for a long, skinny sprinkler).

TEMPORARY REPAIRS
Use electrical tape and this becomes the "bandaid solution."

1   **CLEAN AND DRY THE HOSE.**
Of course, now you can't see where the holes are, so...

2   **PUT ON YOUR BATHING SUIT, TURN ON THE HOSE, LOCATE THE LEAKS, AND USE EITHER A PERMANENT MARKER OR A PIECE OF STRING OR RIBBON (TAPE WON'T STICK) TO MARK THE HOLES.**
Do this on a hot day when the cold water shooting in your face will be a relief, not a shock.

3   **NOW DRY OFF THE HOSE AGAIN, AND STARTING BELOW THE HOLE, WRAP**

ELECTRICAL TAPE OVER THE HOLE BY STRETCHING AND OVERLAPPING IT AS YOU GO.

The stretching and overlapping mean fewer places for the water to squirt out. This is obviously an "if you're in a hurry" method—the crops are dying—but when your bandages begin to spring leaks, it's time for...

PERMANENT REPAIRS

Nothing about your garden hose is permanent if you have someone in your family who insists on mowing it while mowing the lawn or thinks "winter storage" means "under the snow."

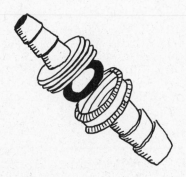

1 **BUY A MALE AND FEMALE COUPLING SET**

or buy as many coupling sets as you have holes. Hoses have a different coupling on each end—1 male, the other female. The female coupling is larger and comes in 3 pieces—the corrugated stem piece, a threaded coupling, and a rubber hose washer. The washer is the "you don't want to lose it" piece; the threaded coupling is the "don't forget to have the stem inserted into it before you put it on the hose" piece; and the corrugated stem is simply the "no good without the other parts" piece. The male coupling is smaller and has no moving parts. Every hose must have 1 male and 1

female end, or they won't connect to anything. The male coupling screws into the female coupling. Sounds like a Biology lesson, or Biology applied to Metallurgy. You could buy a hose repair kit, but in most cases you'd be paying extra for the packaging when all you really need to do is hunt around for the coupling set. **BUY 2 HOSE CLAMPS.**

HELPFUL HINT

This is one of those times when a hint will help you now and could make you angry if you read it at the end. PUT SILICONE CAULKING AROUND THE CORRUGATED METAL STEM OF THE COUPLING TO MAKE IT EASIER TO INSERT INTO THE HOSE AND TO ENSURE THERE WON'T BE A LEAK WHEN YOU TURN ON THE WATER.

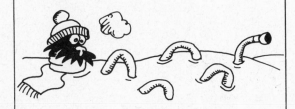

2 **WITH A UTILITY KNIFE, CUT AWAY THE DAMAGED SECTION OF THE HOSE.**
This could be as narrow as the hole or as wide as the lawn mower. **MAKE SURE THE CUTS ARE PERPENDICULAR TO THE LENGTH OF THE HOSE.** Keep trimming until the cuts are clean. **GO SLOWLY—** you'll end up with a longer hose.

3 **SOAK THE END OF THE HOSE IN WARM WATER.**
This makes it easier to insert the coupling; otherwise, it could be like trying to put a round peg into a square hole.

4 **SLIDE 1 CLAMP ONTO EACH PIECE OF HOSE.**
This is definitely the "don't forget" step. If you do forget, you'll be back here at some point, probably when the hose clamp in your hand won't go onto the hose because the coupling is in the way.

5 In case you haven't noticed, you are now dealing with 2 hoses. **HOLD 1 PIECE OF HOSE IN YOUR HAND AND INSERT THE CORRUGATED STEM OF THE COUPLING THAT IS THE OPPOSITE OF THE ONE ON THE OTHER END.**

A piece of hose with the same coupling at each end is not a terribly efficient hose but could be used as a snorkel. **MAKE SURE IT IS SNUGLY SEATED**. If you used the helpful hint, the goop will keep "insert" from becoming "push for all you're worth!"

6 **SLIDE THE HOSE CLAMP UP TO THE COUPLING,**
or if the hose clamp is sitting on the ground looking at you, go back to Steps 4 and 5. **TIGHTEN THE SCREW WITH A SCREW-DRIVER.**

7 **INSERT THE OTHER COUPLING INTO THE OTHER END OF THE HOSE IN THE SAME MANNER.**
If you forgot the hose clamp and it's nowhere to be seen on the hose, it's back to Step 4.

8 **SCREW THE COUPLINGS TOGETHER.**
You have just made 2, 3, or 4 good hoses out of 1 lousy one!

HELPFUL HINTS

How to avoid buying a new hose every spring.

DRAIN AND WIND UP YOUR HOSE AFTER EACH USE. Hoses left on the ground for long periods of time deteriorate.

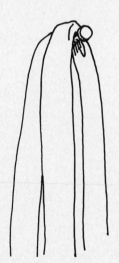

STORE THE HOSE ON A REEL OR COILED ON THE FLOOR. DO NOT HANG IT ON A NAIL; the nail will make a permanent dent in the hose.

BUY A GOOD HOSE WASHER. The washer keeps the water from spurting out of the coupling. A good one stays put inside the female coupling, and a lousy one falls out the minute you disconnect the coupling. Hence, buy several.

NEVER LET WATER FREEZE IN THE HOSE. In other words, drain it and put it away when the weather gets cold. Or if you're making a skating rink, put the hose away when you're finished flooding, or the next time out you'll be in by the fire warming the hose.

Things you learned and might like to remember for next time.

REMOVING AND REPLACING A CERAMIC TILE, AND GROUTING TILES

Something to do on a rainy day when you're confined to the bathroom.

CAULKING A BATHTUB

How to keep the walls around the tub from rotting, or how to save money by not having to replace rotten walls.

1 **DECIDE IF YOU'RE GOING TO USE A SQUEEZE TUBE** (relatively simple) **OR A CAULKING GUN** (relatively difficult without lots of practice) **TO APPLY THE CAULK.**

2 **PURCHASE SILICONE BATHTUB SEALANT THAT IS PERMANENTLY FLEXIBLE, MAKES A WATERPROOF SEAL, IS MILDEW-RESISTANT,** and matches the decor. You only want to do this job once.

3 **REMOVE ALL THE OLD CRACKED CAULK FROM AROUND THE TUB.** You've probably found bits of it having a bath with you lately, or some icky black stuff is growing where the caulk used to be. **USE A WALL SCRAPER WITH CARE SO AS NOT TO SCRATCH THE TUB OR TILES.**

4 **THOROUGHLY CLEAN AND DRY THE SPACE BETWEEN THE TUB AND TILES.** Hair dryers are great for thorough drying— except of course when it comes to your hair.

5 **TO MAKE THE JOB LOOK REALLY PROFESSIONAL** (and I stress the word "look"), **TAPE A STRIP OF MASKING TAPE TO THE TILES, APPROXIMATELY 1/4″ FROM THEIR BASE, AROUND THE TUB WALL.**

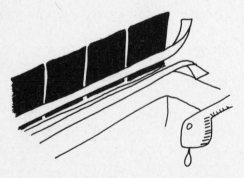

6 **TAPE A SECOND STRIP OF MASKING TAPE TO THE TUB APPROXIMATELY 1/4″ FROM ITS EDGE.** You have just made a channel for the caulk and eliminated the usually messy, undefined edges.

7 **CUT THE NOZZLE OF THE TUBE OR GUN TO THE DESIRED OPENING AT A 45° ANGLE.** How you figure out what is a 45° angle, I'll leave up to you. The size of this opening is determined by the space between the 2 surfaces that you are going to *lap*. What comes out of the nozzle is now called a *bead*, and it must lap both surfaces to make

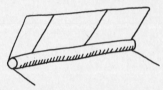

a seal. If the opening is too small, the caulk will just squirt into the crack, seal nothing, and you'll be doing this again in a week.

8 **FILL THE TUB WITH WATER.** Caulking seals are broken because the tub is emptied and filled so often. Filling the tub puts almost maximum weight into the tub and makes the space between the tub and wall almost maximum. If you want to get rid of the "almost," hop in and have a tubbie while you're working. Remember to take off your clothes!

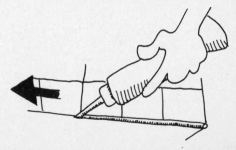

9 **IF YOU CHOSE THE SQUEEZE TUBE,** you're my kind of smart. **SQUEEZE THE TUBE WITH EVEN PRESSURE AND APPLY THE CAULK BY PUSHING THE SEALANT AHEAD OF THE NOZZLE.** This not only pushes the caulk into the space but also laps both surfaces. **TRY**

NOT TO BREAK THE FLOW OF THE CAULK TOO OFTEN; stopping only increases your chances of making a lousy seal. However, it's a long way around the tub, so when you do stop, take a big breath, flex your fingers, and push ahead.

10 **IF YOU CHOSE THE CAULKING GUN** (there must have been a good reason), **SQUEEZE THE RELEASE, PULL BACK ON THE PLUNGER, AND LOAD THE CAULK CARTRIDGE, BACK END FIRST** (the pointed end goes to the front), **INTO THE BARREL OF THE GUN.**

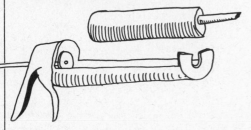

Sounds like war, and it very well might be—between you and the machine.

11 **CUT THE NOZZLE TO THE DESIRED OPENING AT A 45° ANGLE AND PUNCTURE THE INNER SEAL OF THE CARTRIDGE WITH A NAIL OR ANYTHING LONG, SKINNY, AND POINTED.**
If you forget to do this, a blob of caulking will explode when you squeeze the trigger, and the war will begin.

12 **SQUEEZE THE TRIGGER OF THE GUN AND WITH SMOOTH, EVEN PRESSURE APPLY THE SEALANT.**
This does take practice, but if you're determined, find a nice out-of-the-way corner and try it. Don't turn the bathtub into an experiment!

13 **WET YOUR FINGER AND SMOOTH THE NEWLY CAULKED SURFACE IN 2′ SECTIONS.**
Now where do you put the goo that's on your finger? Have a wet rag handy. This, too, will get gooey. Now you have a gooey rag and a gooey finger. You're only halfway around the tub. **LAUGH,** you'll think of something.

14 **REMOVE THE MASKING TAPE.**
The neat, tidy edges will make you feel like a pro.

15 **LET THE CAULK SET FOR 24 HOURS.**
No one gets a bath for 2 days—unless you're desperate, and then it's a good way to meet your neighbor.

Note: Try to use a sealant that cleans up with water.

HELPFUL HINTS
TO MAKE SURE YOU USE ALL THE CAULK IN THE CARTRIDGE, INSERT A GOLF BALL BETWEEN THE CAULKING GUN PLUNGER AND THE CARTRIDGE. SQUEEZE THE TRIGGER AND YOU'LL SQUEEZE EVERY LAST BIT OF GOOP OUT OF THE CARTRIDGE.

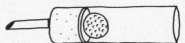

TO SEAL A PARTIALLY USED CARTRIDGE, USE A WIRE CAP.

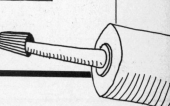

REMOVING AND REPLACING A CERAMIC TILE

Hope you have a replacement tile stashed in the basement.

6 WITH A COLD CHISEL AND A HAMMER, START CHIPPING OUT THE TILE AT THE PUNCHED HOLE, WORKING TO ENLARGE THE HOLE.
Easy does it. You could whack away at the tile, but save your strength—you don't want to damage any adjacent tiles.

7 REMOVE ALL THE TILE IN THIS MANNER.
Slow and steady gets only the damaged tile out and leaves the rest of the wall intact.

8 REMOVE ALL THE OLD GROUT AND ADHESIVE WITH A PUTTY KNIFE OR SCRAPER.

9 WITH A SERRATED (NOTCHED) TROWEL, APPLY TILE ADHESIVE EVENLY TO THE WALL SURFACE AND THE BACK OF THE REPLACEMENT TILE.
For me a little too much is better than a little too little.

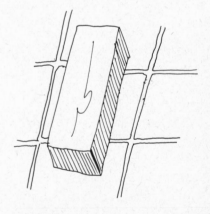

1 PUT ON A PAIR OF SAFETY GLASSES—essential no matter how you look at it.

2 FIND THE CENTER OF THE TILE BY USING A STRAIGHT EDGE AND A MARKER AND DRAWING AN "X" FROM THE CORNERS ACROSS THE TILE.

3 USING A HAMMER AND CENTER PUNCH, NAIL SET, OR PLAIN OLD ORDINARY NAIL, POKE A HOLE THROUGH THE GLAZE IN THE CENTER OF THE DAMAGED TILE.
Be careful not to punch right through the tile and then the wall.

4 USE A METAL STRAIGHT EDGE AND GLASS CUTTER TO HEAVILY SCORE THE GROUT AROUND THE EDGES OF THE TILE.

5 HEAVILY SCORE THE "X" IN STEP 2, if you haven't rubbed it off yet, THROUGH THE HOLE YOU MADE IN THE CENTER OF THE TILE.

10 PUT THE NEW TILE IN PLACE AND HOLD A BLOCK OF WOOD ACROSS IT. TAP THE WOOD WITH A HAMMER UNTIL THE TILE IS FLUSH—even and level—WITH THE ADJACENT TILES.

11 IMMEDIATELY REMOVE THE EXCESS ADHESIVE THAT HAS SQUISHED OUT THE EDGES.

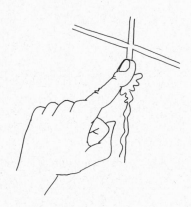

12 LET THE TILE SET FOR 24 HOURS BEFORE GROUTING.
If it's in the bathroom, go away for the weekend.

HELPFUL HINT
IF YOU CAN'T FIND A MATCHING REPLACEMENT TILE, USE A DECORATIVE TILE INSTEAD.

Grout is the white, brown, or grey stuff that fills the cracks between the tiles and makes the entire surface waterproof. It also makes the tiles look pretty.

1 MIX THE POWDERED GROUT WITH WATER ACCORDING TO THE MANUFACTURER'S INSTRUCTIONS.
They say the consistency should be like paste or heavy cream. What kind of paste or cream? Toothpaste? Face cream? Shaving cream? This could also become a mixing marathon. Add water to the stuff and it's too thick. Add more water and it's too thin. Add more stuff and of course you've added too much, so you add more water...ad infinitum. You have now graduated from a small cup to a spaghetti pot trying to arrive at the precise "consistency!"

2 WITH EITHER A RUBBER SQUEEGEE OR *FLOAT* (technical name for one of these), FIRMLY PRESS THE GROUT INTO THE CRACKS.
If you don't fill the cracks, the grout will shrink and split as it dries.

3 FINISH THE CRACKS AND CORNERS WITH THE ERASER OF A PENCIL, A CLOTHESPIN, OR YOUR FINGERS.
Fingers work best, but after a few tiles you run out of fingers. At that point take off your shoes!

4 WIPE OFF THE EXCESS GROUT WITH A CLEAN, WET SPONGE, MAKING SURE THERE IS NO FILM LEFT ON THE TILES.
Do this within 15 minutes of grouting, or the film will be there forever. Do not answer the telephone. Do not answer the doorbell. Do not answer any cries for help.

5 LET THE GROUT DRY FOR 24 HOURS.
If it's tub tiles you've just grouted, don't have a shower right away, or you'll watch the grout run down the drain.

HELPFUL HINT
WHEN MIXING GROUT, ALWAYS ADD WATER TO THE POWDER, NOT VICE VERSA. IT MIXES MORE EASILY AND IS NOT LUMPY.

Things you learned and might like to remember for next time.

WALLPAPER

Also called wall cover-ing because more often than not it isn't paper at all. And you can do it—honest, just laugh a lot!

WALLPAPER DO'S AND DON'TS

"Do" read this first. What you "don't" need is a problem—and that is the understatement of the month!

1 SMILE IF THE FIRST STRIP OF PAPER FALLS OFF THE WALL. THEN GO BACK AND READ THE INSTRUCTIONS.

2 ALWAYS USE A PENCIL TO MARK THE WALLS. PENS, PERMANENT MARKERS, AND COLORED CRAYONS BLEED THROUGH THE PAPER.

3 KEEP CHILDREN AND PETS AWAY FROM THE WATER TRAY OR ADHESIVE. They might drink it, and they will certainly step in it. **IT'S DANGEROUS EITHER WAY.** If anyone steps in it, it might as well be just you.

4 WITH PLAIN OR TEXTURED PAPER, HANG EVERY OTHER STRIP IN REVERSE FOR MORE UNIFORM COLOR. Don't try this with patterned paper.

5 TURN DOWN THE HEAT TO PREVENT TOO RAPID DRYING. Cuddle up with someone.

6 TURN OFF THE POWER TO THE ROOM YOU ARE WORKING IN. WATER IN ELECTRICAL OUTLETS IS DANGEROUS. If you don't know which fuse is which, turn off one you know and wallpaper that room.

7 DON'T USE WALLPAPER PASTE WITH PREPASTED PAPER. THE ADHESIVES MAY NOT BE COMPATIBLE, AND THE PAPER WILL EITHER FALL OFF THE WALL OR BE LUMPY.

HELPFUL HINT
HANG A STRIP OF WALLPAPER IN A WARM, DRY, OUT-OF-THE-WAY PLACE LIKE THE ATTIC OR A CLOSET. IT WILL AGE THE SAME AS THE PAPER YOU'VE HUNG, AND IT CAN BE USED TO MAKE PATCHES FOR THOSE MYSTERIOUS BUT INEVITABLE REPAIRS YOU WILL MAKE.

HANGING PREPASTED WALLPAPER

1 SMILE AND WORK ON YOUR SENSE OF HUMOR.

2 MAKE FRIENDS WITH YOUR DEALER.
A dealer knows how to measure, will tell you how much paper you need, and may even take back the extra roll you should buy just in case.

3 CHECK ALL THE PATTERN AND LOT NUMBERS ON YOUR ORDERED ROLLS.
If they don't match, neither will your walls.

4 READ THE INSTRUCTIONS THOROUGHLY—
not fascinating, but essential.

5 MAKE SURE THE WALLS ARE PROPERLY PREPARED.
If not, the paper will end up on the floor and on you. If you forgot and this happens, go back to Step 1.

6 ENTER THE ROOM AND START ON THE WALL BEHIND YOU.
By the time you get to the wall in front of you, you'll be good at it.

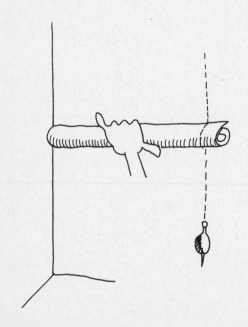

7 MEASURE THE WIDTH OF THE ROLL OF PAPER AND SUBTRACT 1″.

8 MARK THIS MEASUREMENT FROM ONE OF THE CORNERS CLOSE TO THE CEILING ON THE WALL WITH A PENCIL.
Pens, permanent markers, and color crayons bleed through paper.

9 PUT A THUMBTACK INTO THE MARK AND HANG FROM IT A PIECE OF STRING THAT MEASURES JUST SHORT OF THE BASEBOARD. TIE A WEIGHT TO THE STRING—your scissors or house keys. WAIT UNTIL THE WHOLE SHEBANG HOLDS STILL AND MARK THE LINE ALONG THE STRING WITH A PENCIL AND A STRAIGHT EDGE.
Ta-dah! You have just made a plumb line, and all this without a plum. It ensures that the paper goes up straight and not at an angle. **YOU MUST DO THIS ON EVERY WALL.**

10 REMOVE THE PLUMB LINE.
If you don't, you'll have a lump in your wall.

121

11 HIKE UP THE LADDER, PAPER IN HAND, AND HOLD THE PAPER AT THE CEILING. LEAVE 2" OR 3" EXTRA AT THE TOP— this is called a *trim margin*—AND ROLL THE PAPER DOWN THE WALL.
You'll discover that your arms and feet only reach so far, so make sure there's nothing below. You'll have to drop the roll to the floor at some point.

12 LEAVE 2" OR 3" EXTRA AT THE BASE-BOARD, for trim margin, AND CUT THE STRIP.

13 REROLL THE STRIP FROM THE BOTTOM UP.
The outside end goes up to the ceiling. This is extremely important if your paper has birds or flowers on it. You don't want them hanging upside down.

14 FILL THE WATER TRAY HALF FULL WITH WARM WATER AND PLACE THE TRAY AT THE BASEBOARD DIRECTLY UNDER WHERE YOU WILL HANG THE FIRST STRIP.

15 PLACE THE CUT, ROLLED-UP STRIP INTO THE WATER AND LET IT SOAK EVENLY FOR THE TIME THE DIREC-TIONS SPECIFY.
Do not use the bathtub for a trough unless you're papering directly over it—it's a long, sticky walk back to the wall.

16 PULL THE PAPER SLOWLY FROM THE TRAY UP TO THE CEILING.
Stay clear of the wall. You now have a huge ᐟ piece of flypaper in your hands—remember Step 1.

17 LINE UP THE EDGE OF THE PAPER WITH THE PENCIL LINE. AND DON'T BE AFRAID TO HANDLE THE PAPER.
You have about 5 minutes to wiggle it around.

18 WITH A WET SPONGE, preferably one that looks like this

SMOOTH OUT THE STRIP, WORKING DOWN THE CENTER AND OUT TO THE EDGES.
Remove the large air bubbles, but do not overwork the edges—you'll squish out all the adhesive.

19 TRIM OFF THE EXCESS PAPER (your trim margin) AT THE TOP AND BOTTOM OF THE STRIP WITH EITHER WALLPAPER SHEARS OR A METAL STRAIGHT EDGE AND AN EXTRA-SHARP UTILITY KNIFE.
Hold the straight edge so that the metal edge butts up snugly to the ceiling or base-board and cut into the ceiling and baseboard

as you trim. "Into" means "toward." This eliminates the possibility of gouging the gorgeous strip of paper you have just hung and Step 1 coming into play.

20 **TAKE A BIG BREATH, CROSS YOUR FINGERS, STEP BACK, AND ADMIRE YOUR HANDIWORK.**

21 **PROCEED TO HANG THE SECOND STRIP BY MATCHING THE PATTERN AGAINST THE FIRST STRIP YOU APPLIED.**
You may have to waste several inches of paper, but the manufacturer has allowed for this and has given you extra. Remember, match the heads of the birds with the tails of the birds.

22 **REPEAT STEPS 11 TO 16.**
You can skip putting clean water in the tray until you've hung 6 to 8 strips, unless of course you've stepped in the tray and spilled all the water.

23 **BUTT THE EDGE OF STRIP 2 TO THE EDGE OF STRIP 1, MATCHING THE PATTERN.**
Do not overlap the edges.

24 **REPEAT STEPS 18 TO 20.**
Doesn't it drive you crazy when you have to go back and reread steps? But Step 20 is especially important, as it will give you the incentive to continue.

25 **KEEP GOING IN THE SAME MANNER UNTIL YOU COME TO A CORNER.**
At this point you may decide that the room needs only 1 papered wall. You might want to quit while you're ahead. Don't panic if the edges don't look well stuck or if there are a few small air bubbles. Drying seems to make everything look better.

OR IF ALL ELSE FAILS: HELPFUL HINT
USE WHITE GLUE TO STICK DOWN WALLPAPER EDGES ALONG SEAMS THAT REFUSE TO STAY STUCK.

WALLPAPERING AN INSIDE CORNER

Where the fun begins.

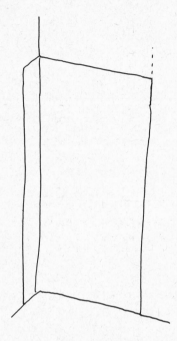

1 MEASURE THE DISTANCE BETWEEN THE EDGE OF YOUR LAST STRIP AND THE CORNER. ADD 1″

and write it down. You'll forget if you don't. This extra will extend around the corner and allow for any unevenness of the wall.

2 MEASURE AND CUT THE STRIP AS BEFORE,
Steps 11 and 12.

3 USING THE MEASUREMENT YOU MADE IN STEP 1, MARK THE ENTIRE LENGTH OF THE STRIP WITH A PENCIL AND CUT TO THE REQUIRED WIDTH.
At this point you can be thankful that you don't have 14′ ceilings, or if you do, **SMILE!**

4 SAVE THE PIECE YOU HAVE JUST CUT OFF.
It goes on the adjoining wall, believe it or not.

5 APPLY THE MEASURED PIECE AS BEFORE.

6 MEASURE AND MARK ON THE ADJOINING WALL THE WIDTH OF THE STRIP SAVED IN STEP 4.
If you rumpled it up and threw it in the garbage or it has just simply disappeared, improvise.

7 AT THIS MARK DROP A PLUMB LINE AND MARK IT WITH A PENCIL.

8 APPLY THIS STRIP OF PAPER BY LINING UP THE EDGE WITH THE PLUMB LINE MARK. ALLOW THE OTHER EDGE TO GO INTO THE CORNER.
The plumb line and the edges in the corner will fix any crooked corners. If the paper doesn't match in the corner, don't worry. That's the way it's supposed to be—honest. If you want it to match in the corner, be creative!

WALLPAPERING AN OUTSIDE CORNER

1 **WRAP THE STRIP AROUND THE CORNER.**
Hooray, something sorta simple! Too bad they don't make rooms with all outside corners.

2 **SNIP THE CORNER OVERHANG AT THE CEILING AND BASEBOARD.**
This allows the paper to go around the other wall easily.

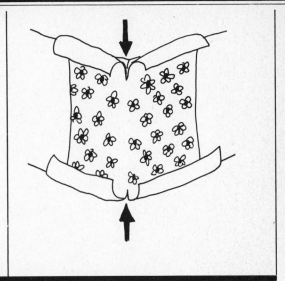

WALLPAPERING AROUND DOORS, WINDOWS, SWITCH PLATES, WALL FIXTURES, ETC.

1 **WHEN YOU COME TO AN OBSTRUCTION, PAPER RIGHT OVER IT.**
Don't try to cut the paper to fit around things, or you'll drive yourself crazy. If you didn't like whatever it is in the first place, don't bother to cut it out at all.

2 **MAKE DIAGONAL CUTS UP TO AND SLIGHTLY BEYOND THE CORNERS.**

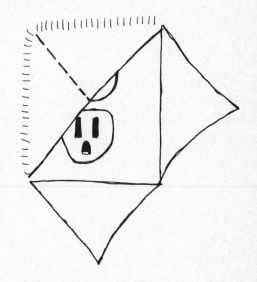

3 **TRIM THE EXCESS PAPER WITH A STRAIGHT EDGE AND SHARP UTILITY KNIFE.**

PATCHING WALLPAPER

This is the double-cut method, essential for divots large and small and any slight miscalculations you made when first putting up the paper.

1 **CUT A SQUARE PATCH TO OVERLAP THE DAMAGED AREA BY ABOUT 1″.** Squares are easier to handle than circles.

2 **POSITION THE PATCH OVER THE DAMAGED AREA AND ALIGN THE PATTERN *EXACTLY* ON ALL SIDES.** Remember, the idea is to keep the patch from looking like a mistake.

3 **SECURE THE PATCH AT THE CORNERS WITH EITHER MASKING TAPE OR THUMBTACKS.** Be careful—masking tape might mar the paper, and you'll be making a bigger patch.

4 **USING A METAL STRAIGHT EDGE AND SHARP KNIFE, CUT CLEANLY THROUGH BOTH LAYERS OF PAPER ON ALL SIDES OF THE SECTION.**

5 **REMOVE THE PATCH.**

6 **GO OVER THE CUTS ON THE DAMAGED SECTION WITH YOUR KNIFE TO MAKE SURE THAT THE EDGES ARE SEPARATED—** a potential "why bother" step, but who wants to make a bigger patch?

7 **WITH YOUR KNIFE BLADE, PRY UP 1 CORNER OF THE CUT AREA, AND THE DAMAGED SECTION SHOULD COME OUT IN 1 PIECE.** Good luck. If it doesn't all come out, don't give up. Use a putty knife to scrape any remaining bits of paper, glue, and/or lumps off the wall. This is where elbow grease meets wallpaper paste.

8 **IF THE PATCH IS PREPASTED, WET IT AND SHAKE OFF THE EXCESS WATER. INSERT THE TOP EDGE INTO THE CLEANED-OUT SECTION AND LET THE PATCH FALL INTO PLACE. PRESS IT DOWN LIGHTLY WITH A CLEAN, DAMP SPONGE.** Don't crease the patch and check to make sure you haven't put the pattern upside down. If you do either, it's back to Step 1.

9 **WAIT A FEW MINUTES AND PRESS AGAIN WITH A CLEAN SPONGE TO MAKE SURE THE PAPER IS GOOD AND STUCK.**

Note: I like the clean sponge requirement. Have you ever tried to find one in your house?

HANGING "YOU PASTE IT" WALLPAPER

REMOVING OLD WALLPAPER

This is basically the same as hanging prepasted paper, except that you replace the sponge with a flat plastic scraper, and all the water-tray steps are replaced with you, a brush, wallpaper adhesive, lots of smiles and laughs, and a good workout for your sense of humor.

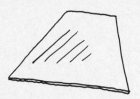

It is essential to talk to your dealer. A dealer will tell you which adhesive to use, sell you the scraper, and if you smile show you how to use the seam roller you'll need.

This could be Step 1 for wallpapering and painting. It should be the easiest form of wallpapering—unwallpapering. It isn't.

Wallpapering over paper is always risky. The water used for prepasted papers and wallpaper adhesive could loosen old layers of paper, and you'll end up with all your newly hung paper in a heap at your feet.

1 **IF YOU KNOW WHAT YOUR WALLS ARE MADE OF, GO ON TO STEP 3.**
How's that for a Step 1?

2 **DETERMINE WHAT THE WALL BENEATH THE PAPER IS MADE OF BY DRILLING A TINY HOLE IN THE WALL.**
If the drill bit produces white dust and moderate resistance to the drill, the wall is made of plaster. Brown dust and moderate resistance followed by a "pop" means the wall is made of wood or a wood product. A spray of water means you hit a pipe; turn to the plumbing section. White dust, little resistance, and a quick drill "pop" mean drywall. If you think you hit a stud, move the drill 6″ to 8″ away on a diagonal and try again. If you know you hit a stud, you don't need this book!

HELPFUL HINT
NEVER WALLPAPER WITH YOUR SPOUSE OR SOMEONE YOU LIKE A LOT OR EVER WANT TO SPEAK TO AGAIN.

IF THE WALLS ARE MADE OF PLASTER OR WOOD, THE OLD WALL COVERING CAN BE SOAKED OFF. IF THE WALLS ARE MADE OF DRYWALL, YOU MUST DRY-STRIP THE PAPER.
Water wrecks drywall and your surprise for the day will be replacing the wall.

DRY-STRIPPING WALLPAPER

1 TO DRY-STRIP THE WALL, BORROW A STRIPPER—
not a person, but a specific tool.

2 HOLD THE BLADE OF THE STRIPPER PERPENDICULAR TO THE WALL AND APPLY GENTLE PRESSURE.

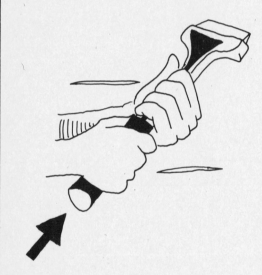

3 SLIT THE PAPER HORIZONTALLY EVERY 8″ to 10″ AND SLIDE THE BLADE UNDER THE SLIT AT AN ANGLE.
Be careful. You're not digging a ditch or you'll create a new project.

4 LOOSEN THE SECTION OF PAPER AND TEAR IT OFF WITH YOUR FINGERS.
Look around you and wish the room were smaller.

1 WET THE OLD PAPER BY FIRST ROUGHENING THE SURFACE WITH COARSE SANDPAPER OR A WIRE BRUSH.
This allows slick or nonporous paper to accept the water.

2 WITH A LARGE SPONGE, WET A STRIP OF PAPER WITH HOT WATER AND A MILD DETERGENT TO SOFTEN THE OLD PASTE.
You could use a chemical stripper for stubborn paper, and definitely use a sponge mop or paint roller for high-up places. Take off your shoes and wear a raincoat!

3 LET THE STRIP SOAK FOR 10 MINUTES.

4 RESOAK THIS STRIP AND WET STRIP 2.

5 WHILE WAITING FOR THE WATER TO PENETRATE STRIP 2, MOP THE FLOOR AND GO BACK TO STRIP 1.

6 WITH A 3″-WIDE WALL SCRAPER HELD AT A 45° ANGLE FROM THE WALL, FIRMLY PUSH THE PAPER UP FROM THE BOTTOM.
The paper should wrinkle up like an accordion. If it doesn't, resoak the strip and try again, and again, and…

7 **GRASP THE LOOSENED PAPER AND TEAR UPWARD IN A STEADY MOTION.** Don't hurry or you could end up with only a tiny scrap of paper in your hand.

8 **RESOAK STRIP 2 AND WET STRIP 3. REMOVE STRIP 2 AND WHAT'S LEFT OF STRIP 1,** if you can remember which is which. Maybe number them. And so it goes around the room. That's the bad news.

9 **AFTER STRIPPING OFF ALL THE PAPER, WASH DOWN THE WALLS TO REMOVE ALL EXCESS GOOP.** The good news is you don't have to take a shower; you've just had one!

Invariably it's the worn spot that appears directly in front of the bathroom sink. I don't know why. Maybe everyone jogs here while brushing their teeth, or maybe it's one of those particular spots where objects hit the floor repeatedly—hair dryers, curling irons, electric shavers. And of course there comes a day when you hook your toe under the edge of the flooring, so you relocate the bathmat from in front of the tub to in front of the sink; you remember the hole when it comes time to wash the mat. You'd better do something while the patch still has a chance of resembling the old flooring and you're inspired by the idea of doing such a good job that no one will notice. Grab the bath mat—they'll notice that's gone for sure—throw it into the washing machine, and get busy, relieved that at the moment you aren't replacing a floor.

1 **HUNT AROUND AND FIND THAT EXTRA PIECE OF FLOORING YOU SAVED WHEN YOU PUT THE FLOOR IN 5 YEARS AGO.**
Of course, for 4 of those 5 years you tripped over that extra piece every second day. Now it can be a full hour of looking in all those safekeeping places. Why do so many things end up under a child's bed?

2 **CUT A SQUARE PATCH OUT OF THIS PIECE OF FLOORING, AT LEAST 4" LARGER ON ALL SIDES THAN THE DAMAGED AREA.**

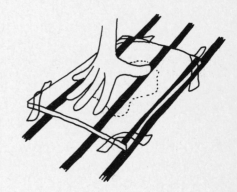

3 **PLACE THE PATCH OVER THE DAMAGED AREA AND MATCH THE PATTERN EXACTLY AT THE EDGES.**
This "exact" part makes it harder for anyone to notice your handiwork.

4 **TAPE THE PATCH IN PLACE WITH MASKING TAPE.**

5 **USE A UTILITY KNIFE AND METAL STRAIGHT EDGE TO CUT THROUGH BOTH THE PATCH AND THE DAMAGED FLOORING.**
Cutting along pattern lines helps conceal the patch. This takes a certain amount of strength, so don't be in a hurry. When you stop to let the blood in your hand recirculate, do it without removing the knife from the cut. Just give your fingers a wiggle.

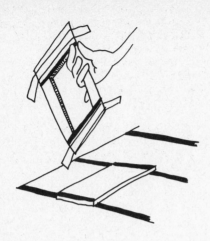

8 **USE A SCRAPER OR PUTTY KNIFE TO PRY UP THE SOFTENED FLOORING, WORKING FROM THE CENTER OF THE DAMAGED AREA TO ITS EDGES.**
If this doesn't work, you could use a hammer and chisel, but be careful not to dig up a hunk of the subfloor.

6 **REMOVE THE PATCH AND DON'T BE SURPRISED IF THE DAMAGED FLOORING DOESN'T LIFT OFF THE FLOOR.**
It probably won't. If it doesn't, Steps 7 and 8 are for you.

9 **SCRAPE ANY OLD ADHESIVE OFF THE FLOOR.**
If you leave it there, you are guaranteed 1 lumpy patch. Everyone will notice—bare feet are terrific lump detectors.

7 **COVER THE DAMAGED AREA WITH A DAMP CLOTH, AND WITH A WARM IRON GO OVER THE AREA TO SOFTEN THE TILE AND THE ADHESIVE THAT'S HOLDING WHAT'S LEFT OF THE DAMAGED FLOOR IN PLACE.**

10 **CHECK THE FIT OF THE PATCH.**
If you goofed while cutting, you could sand the patch a bit or shave and edge it with a utility knife. Just be careful; you can't make a too-small patch bigger.

11 SPREAD A THIN LAYER OF FLOORING ADHESIVE, NOT MORE THAN HALF THE THICKNESS OF THE FLOORING, ON THE SUBFLOOR WITH A NOTCHED TROWEL.

12 PUT THE PATCH IN PLACE, MAKING SURE IT IS LEVEL WITH THE ADJACENT FLOORING.

If it isn't, press down on the patch until it is level, then immediately wipe off the excess goop that squishes out from the edges. If the patch is too low, lift it and put more adhesive on the subfloor.

13 COVER THE PATCH WITH A PIECE OF WOOD AND WEIGHT IT DOWN WITH SOMETHING THAT WEIGHS AT LEAST 20 POUNDS—a child, a dog, books—UNTIL THE ADHESIVE IS THOROUGHLY DRY.

If you have none of these, make yourself comfortable and stand on it.

14 **TO HIDE THE OUTLINE OF THE PATCH, COVER ITS EDGES WITH A PIECE OF HEAVY ALUMINUM FOIL, DULL SIDE DOWN, AND PRESS THE FOIL SEVERAL TIMES WITH A VERY HOT IRON.**
Stand back and admire your lovely floor. Put a "Notice Anything?" sign on the bathroom mirror. Bet they don't! The bathmat can now go back to its place in front of the tub.

HELPFUL HINTS

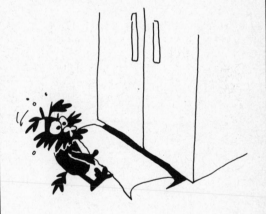

IF YOU DON'T HAVE AN EXTRA PIECE OF FLOORING, USE A PIECE FROM UNDER THE REFRIGERATOR OR INSIDE A CLOSET.

YOU CAN LINE DRAWERS WITH A PIECE OF LEFTOVER FLOORING.

CHAIR REPAIR

*When sitting on something
other than the floor
is essential.*

REWEBBING LAWN FURNITURE

Get organized for the first suntanning day of the summer. Send the kids off on a bike picnic. Wonder why your bathing suit looked better last summer. Give up looking for the tanning lotion and settle for baby oil. Make yourself a nice glass of iced tea. Drag last summer's lawn chair out of the garage. Open it and face it toward the sun; after all, suntanning is a science. Smile and sit down, close your eyes, pretend that the ripping sound you hear is only the material getting used to being outside once again. All of a sudden you realize that you're on your way out of the chair, through the seat. Jump up and laugh. Never mind, you'll get a tan anyway. You'll just get it sitting on the ground while you fix the chair!

1 **DECIDE HOW MUCH OF THE WEBBING MUST BE REPLACED.**
If your only concern is having something to sit on, you only have to replace the damaged straps. If you really want to make the chair look almost new, you can reweb the entire chair. It's not difficult, it's not expensive, and you'll be doing 2 things at once—fixing the chair and getting a tan. Both you and the chair will look gorgeous.

2 **CAREFULLY REMOVE THE DAMAGED STRAPS BY PRYING THE CLIPS AT EITHER END OF EACH STRAP FREE WITH A SCREWDRIVER. KEEP ONE OF THE DAMAGED STRAPS INTACT.**
You'll need it not only for a pattern but also for a measurement.

3 **MEASURE THE LENGTH OF THE STRAP AND COUNT THE NUMBER OF STRAPS YOU ARE GOING TO REPLACE.**
If you're good at measuring, counting, and adding, you'll know how much new webbing to buy. If you measure like I do, buy extra!

4 **MAKE A QUICK TRIP TO THE STORE.**
You need a few minutes out of the sun at some point; it might as well be now. **BUY EITHER A REPAIR KIT,** if it's available, **OR ENOUGH POLYPROPYLENE WEBBING,** the flat, woven, see-through stuff, **TO FIX THE CHAIR. BUY EITHER C-CLIPS OR WASHER-HEAD SCREWS TO ATTACH THE WEBBING.** C-clips are easier to use; read Steps 7 and 8 and decide for yourself. **IF YOU DECIDE TO REWEB THE CHAIR WITH SOLID PLASTIC WEBBING, BUY SHEET-METAL SCREWS** (if they don't

come in the package with the webbing) **TO ATTACH THIS WEBBING TO THE CHAIR FRAME.** Step 9 tells you how to do it. If you have any difficulty deciding what's best for your chair and/or reading these directions, ask the person at the store. You'll probably have to ask where the C-clips are anyway. **IF YOU THINK THE HELPFUL HINT SOUNDS LIKE A GOOD IDEA, BUY SOME AUTOMOBILE PASTE WAX.** While you're out, get some suntan lotion.

HELPFUL HINT
This hint will help you now, and it will definitely do nothing for you or your chair at the end of this section.

BEFORE REWEBBING AN ALUMINUM CHAIR, CLEAN THE FRAME WITH A SOAP-FILLED KITCHEN SCOURING PAD AND COAT THE FRAME WITH CAR WAX. Who needs new webbing if the frame decays?

5 Put on the tanning lotion and head back into the sunshine with a new glass of iced tea, the stuff you bought at the store, and a pair

of scissors. **CUT THE NEW WEBBING INTO STRAPS THE SAME LENGTH AS THE OLD STRAPS.**
The strap in Step 2 is now a pattern.

6 **TO REPLACE ALL THE CHAIR WEBBING, BEGIN WITH THE FIRST HORIZONTAL** (crosswise) **STRAP AT THE TOP OF THE CHAIR BACK. DO ALL THE HORIZONTAL STRAPS FIRST.**

7 **IF THE REPLACEMENT WEBBING IS POLYPROPYLENE AND IS TO BE ATTACHED WITH WASHER-HEAD SCREWS, FOLD IN BOTH CORNERS AT 1 END OF THE STRAP LIKE THIS**

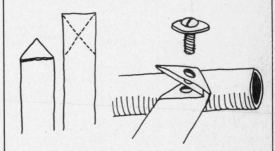

TO FORM A POINT AT ITS CENTER. USE AN AWL TO POKE A HOLE THROUGH ALL 4 THICKNESSES OF WEBBING. FASTEN 1 END OF THE STRAP TO THE HOLE IN THE FRAME WITH A SCREW AND ATTACH THE OTHER END IN THE SAME WAY.
This is a bit tricky, and be careful not to poke yourself with the awl.

8 IF THE WEBBING IS TO BE ATTACHED WITH C-CLIPS, LAP 3/4" OF THE WEBBING OVER THE CLIP AT 1 END OF THE STRAP AND SNAP THE CLIP OVER THE FRAME. REPEAT THIS AT THE OTHER END OF THE STRAP.
See? Easy as pie! You have just read 2 steps that may come in handy if you repair your mother-in-law's lawn chair.

9 IF THE WEBBING IS SOLID PLASTIC, THE PACKAGE OF WEBBING WILL ALSO CONTAIN FLAT METAL BARS WITH A HOLE IN THEIR CENTERS. PLACE A BAR AT THE END OF THE STRAP AND FOLD THE STRAP AND THE BAR OVER ONCE. WITH AN AWL,

MAKE A HOLE THROUGH BOTH PIECES OF PLASTIC TO CORRESPOND WITH THE HOLE IN THE METAL BAR. SCREW THIS TO THE HOLE IN THE CHAIR FRAME WITH A SHEET METAL SCREW.
Be careful when you're busy poking holes in the plastic. Awls are sharp, pointed things that have a habit of poking fingers, especially mine.

10 ATTACH 1 END OF EACH VERTICAL (lengthwise) STRAP TO THE FRAME AND WEAVE THEM ALTERNATELY OVER AND UNDER THE ALREADY SECURED HORIZONTAL STRAPS. MAKE SURE EACH STRAP GOES BEHIND THE BAR AT THE BACK OF THE SEAT. ATTACH THE FREE ENDS OF THE VERTICAL STRAPS TO THE FRAME.

11 Now for the fun part. **SMILE. ADMIRE YOUR LOVELY CHAIR AND SLOWLY SIT DOWN IN IT. CLOSE YOUR EYES.** You're still in the chair. **SIP YOUR ICED TEA.** You aren't going anywhere. **HOORAY, YOU DID IT!**
You have more to show off than just a tan. Then you hear a sound—the kids are home!

REPAIRING A WOODEN CHAIR WITH GLUE

Glue is the quickest, least complicated, tool-free, and best way to repair a wiggly chair, other than buying a new one. I have chairs in various stages of coming apart. They live at the kitchen table. One day someone who weighs slightly more than the child for whom the chair is designated sits down, way down, on the floor. It's time to move my friend to the Daddy Bear's chair and reassemble the pieces. In fact, I have a stool reserved for those 48-hour periods when the glue is drying. Funny how much use I get out of that stool, and it always seems to get used after I've had a house guest!

1 COVER THE WORK SURFACE WITH NEWSPAPER OR A PLASTIC DROP CLOTH—
glue drips. If your friend is going to hang around and watch, you can work at the kitchen table.

2 THOROUGHLY CLEAN ANY OLD GLUE OFF THE PIECES THAT ARE TO BE JOINED TOGETHER WITH A SLOTTED SCREWDRIVER OR BLUNT CHISEL—
the only kind I have. Just be careful not to gouge the wood. If you use a knife, shave off the glue, not the wood. **USE SANDPAPER** if the old glue is really stuck or try soaking the piece in warm white vinegar to loosen the glue.

3 MAKE SURE THE PIECES TO BE GLUED ARE DRY.
If you used the vinegar trick, your friend will have to come back later to see the gluing part. **IF THE SURFACES TO BE GLUED ARE SMOOTH, ROUGHEN THEM BY LIGHTLY SCORING THEM WITH A KNIFE.**

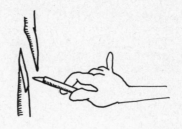

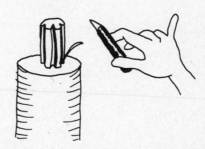

4 MAKE A DRY RUN AT PUTTING THE PIECES TOGETHER.
This is essential because it not only reminds you how the chair goes back together, but it also gives you a chance to figure out how you're going to clamp it after it's glued. **MAKE SURE ALL THE JOINTS FIT SNUGLY.**

5 IF THE JOINT HAS NO GAPS, APPLY WHITE GLUE OR CARPENTER'S GLUE TO BOTH SURFACES AND FORCE THEM TOGETHER.

Always use more glue than you need; the excess will squish out of the joint when pressure is applied. If you are gluing an end-grain piece, use a little more glue; end-grain surfaces absorb more glue than flat surfaces.

6 IF THE JOINT HAS SMALL GAPS, MIX A LITTLE SAWDUST WITH THE GLUE TO MAKE A FILLER.

Glue is not a filler. It just gets absorbed by the wood, and you'll still be left with the gaps and a wiggly joint. **APPLY FILLER TO BOTH SURFACES BEFORE FORCING THEM TOGETHER.**

7 CLAMP THE JOINT TO FORCE THE GLUE INTO THE WOOD FIBERS.

You could use C-clamps if they fit, a web clamp if you have one, or a wood clamp, which also falls into the "if you have one" category. Me, I'd rather make a tourniquet with rope, old clothesline, or pantyhose. It's essential to clamp the joint; otherwise, the glue will not lock the wood fibers in a strong bond. Gluing without clamping is like hammering without a nail.

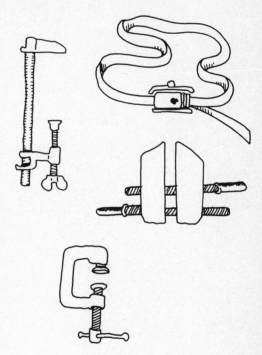

8 WIPE OFF ALL THE EXCESS GLUE WITH A DAMP CLOTH.

White glue not only makes a good, solid joint, but it is also water-soluble. I love anything that can be cleaned up with water!

9 | LET THE CLAMPED JOINT DRY FOR 48 HOURS.

This is where that stool comes in handy. I'm convinced that kids would rather sit on a stool than a chair anyway. They'd probably be happiest sitting on a ladder!

10 | REMOVE THE CLAMP, PUT THE CHAIR BACK WHERE IT BELONGS, AND SIT ON IT. FEEL GOOD KNOWING THAT THE JOINT YOU'VE MADE WILL PROBABLY OUTLAST THE WOOD.

You can invite your friend over again knowing he won't end up sitting on the floor, unless of course he sits on another chair!

HELPFUL HINTS

IF YOUR CHAIR SKIDS ALONG THE FLOOR, GLUE RUBBER HOSE WASHERS TO THE BOTTOM OF EACH LEG.

IF 1 CHAIR LEG IS SHORTER THAN THE OTHERS, GLUE A RUBBER HOSE WASHER TO THE BOTTOM OF THE SHORTER LEG TO STEADY THE CHAIR. This sure beats having to saw off any of the good legs.

TO REPAIR A CHAIR RUNG IF THE JOINT HAS GAPS, COAT A PIECE OF THREAD OR THIN STRING WITH GLUE AND WRAP IT AROUND THE END OF THE RUNG THAT IS TO BE INSERTED INTO A SOCKET. This fills the gaps and makes a solid joint.